simply
contemporary

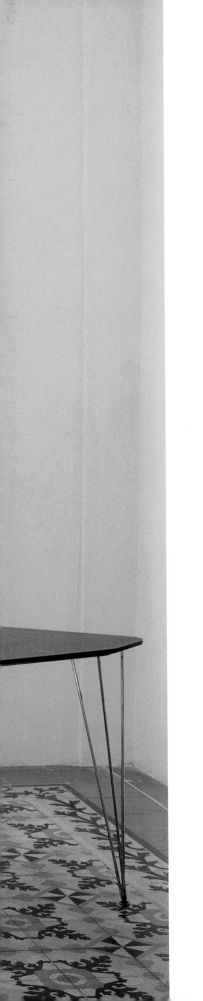

simply contemporary

inspirations for the modern home

solvi dos santos · text by henrietta thompson

CLARKSON POTTER / PUBLISHERS

New York

introduction

Everyone is familiar with the show-home aesthetic – that sharp, clean, expensive and uniform stage-set for the perfect 'lifestyle'. It exists to be shown off and photographed, and it is depicted everywhere – in advertisements, coffee-table books and magazines. In this aspirational world, the home has become little more than a trophy, a symbol of a commercially idealized existence. Thankfully, there are alternatives, and it is these that have inspired this book.

Photographer Solvi dos Santos has seen thousands of beautiful houses on her travels across the world, but often the most interesting – and almost always the most genuinely appealing – are those that are true expressions of the people who live in them. Theirs are the houses that are homes – soulful, uplifting spaces that are the antithesis of off-the-peg perfection. What is more, none of these properties has been made this way through exorbitant budgets, extravagant shopping sprees, armies of assistants or pages of style tips from glossy magazines.

Some of the spaces here have been gutted, rebuilt, left alone, adapted, or simply, in some cases, decorated. Interior designers have not featured unless they are the homeowners themselves and, on the whole, the only 'professional' advice sought is that from friends and family. The ethos is perfectly encapsulated by Anna Bonde, who, although friends and visitors to her farmhouse in Provence are forever asking if she will redesign and redecorate their houses in the same style as she has done her own, says: 'I can't do this for someone else – it takes me years to do it just in my own house. And to make it like this I have to work with what I have. You can't fake it. Interior decoration is too personal.' Maureen Doherty, whose beautiful London apartment is featured, agrees, 'I hate interior designers and architects! They say "You should cover this, or do that," and I just say: "why?".... One's house should always represent one's personality.'

'Simply Contemporary' constitutes a movement of sorts, in which the focus is shifted towards what can come about when people question the real value of objects around them. Rather than the surface minimalism that's so readily available to buy, these homes show that true simplicity can be found through repairing, refurbishing, adapting and recycling the possessions you own and love, and rejecting excess.

Preceding pages: Susanne Rützou's decorated cupboard, in the living room of her flat in Copenhagen (left); a room to relax in, next to the bedroom in Stein Thunberg and IngerLise Hansen's home in Norway (above, right); one of the children's bedrooms in Michael and Marlou Smit's house near Amsterdam (right, centre); a collection of plates in Maureen Doherty's London kitchen (below, right).

This page: Béatrice Courmont's home in Ibiza consists of three separate buildings. From left to right, shelves in her outdoor kitchen and dining room; a collection of family photographs in the bathroom; the kitchen in the main house.

Opposite: The dining area in Chris Lehrecke and Gabriella Kiss's converted church in the Hudson Valley near New York.

This resourceful – and often more eco-conscious – approach to living is refreshing in a time when we've never had so much to consume, nor been so ready to consume it. In such an environment, even a little austerity can be instantly calming, which is not to say that the homes depicted here are severe in their minimalism, however. A house stuffed with treasures can have much the same calming effect, because each object is there for a reason and tells a story, reflecting a life full of emotion and experience. Much of the beauty in the following homes comes from the art of a good display: in the arrangement of old pieces of crockery and shells, junk-shop furniture mixed with exquisite French antiques, or driftwood lined up tidily next to an old milk urn. It is probably no coincidence that many of the homeowners featured are antique dealers, shop owners, artists and designers, but what they have in common is the ability to celebrate beauty in the ordinary, and to elevate an object to a higher status purely by showing how much they love and value it themselves.

By the nature of this 'Simply Contemporary' style of living, all the homes in this book are totally distinct from each other; all are at once both global and local. From a pair of architects who've made a tranquil yet disciplined live-work haven in a rented loft on one of New York's busiest intersections to a writer and intellectual whose decadent hideaway in the shadow of Palma's cathedral was once his family home, but has now become his inspiration, there is poetry in all of them.

a theatrical apartment in berlin

Select pieces of vintage furniture (above) look especially glamorous set against the brightly painted walls. The 1970s glass-topped dining table (opposite), with a collection of red chairs that Fiona found in a refuse collection sales point in Berlin, provides a colourful and playful place to sit in the kitchen. A poster from one of the designer's hat collections hangs on the far wall.

Fiona Bennett's apartment is unusually large for central Berlin. It needs to be, however, given that she shares it not only with her son, Linus, but – and here's another unusual aspect to the flat – also a guinea pig, a turtle and a crayfish.

A talented and successful milliner, Fiona has been creating extravagant and fabulous hats since 1988. With due flair and flamboyance, her reputation for dressing the heads of actors, artists and photographers extends to New York, Milan and Tokyo.

Fiona found a suitable space and established her hat salon in Berlin in 1997 and moved into the apartment in 2002, choosing it partly for its proximity to her shop, partly for its size and partly for the neighbourhood. It is situated in the hub of East Berlin, an area that is thriving, with good shops, as well as small fashionable cafés and galleries.

'It is a young and exciting area,' says Fiona. 'Almost all of our friends and lots of creative people live nearby. I love it and it's so convenient because I can just walk out the door and I am right in the middle of it all.'

Fiona's apartment is decorated in the same theatrical spirit as her salon, which has appropriately dramatic

lighting, striking mint and lilac walls and a luscious red velvet sofa. Elegance and humour are two strong themes that pervade the spaces she lives and works in as much as they do her hats.

'I like strong colours and clear shapes,' she says. 'I am always striving to find the absolute design expression – just to the point – and I love colour. I think a joie de vivre and sense of humour is so important in life, and in my work.'

The Bennetts, with their assorted animals, were the first to move into the house following a careful renovation of the building. On the third floor of a large townhouse built in 1900, it has splendidly high ceilings and all the original doors and windows are intact.

Even the old parquet is still in place, just as it was at the turn of the last century, while the advantage of being on the third floor means that the two balconies offer amazing views over the old city.

Berlin apartments often follow a traditional layout, with the kitchen in the centre. This particular one is no different and four other rooms lead out from this central hub. Three of these are bedrooms and one is a sitting

room. The rest of the flat comprises two bathrooms, two corridors and a dressing room.

The wooden floors have been simply varnished and the ceilings are white, keeping the sense of space and light, but the walls of the flat immediately lend the space an air of drama. The corridor is scarlet, the main bedroom a hot fuchsia pink and the kitchen a strong anis green. Painting it in her customarily confident colours helped Fiona make sense of this very static layout. 'This lets the structure breathe,' she explains.

Fiona has a passion for vintage furniture and has accumulated a wonderful collection of treasured pieces over the years. Although she never sticks rigidly to one period, the designer does favour particular styles and colours and the apartment is for the most part furnished with Art Deco finds from the 1930s and retro 1960s and 1970s finds. 'I like to mix these all together to create my own personal style,' she says.

One particular favourite is her old wooden optician's desk, found for Fiona by her brother, who was dealing in antiques at the time. But beyond that, she says, everything in the apartment is cherished, from the collection of red plastic chairs with chrome feet in

the kitchen, which she found in a vintage shop, to the little art deco occasional table in her bedroom.

'I also love the table from the 1970s with a glass top and chrome circle base – it came from the Berlin's refuse company, which has a special sales point in Berlin.'

Almost as much as her hats, which can be seen, along with their distinctive black-and-white boxes, in the apartment, Fiona is well known for staging glittering shows and flamboyant events. And that, she says, is the very best thing about her apartment: 'You can have a party in the front and can sleep in the back without hearing any noise…'

Just as in Fiona's salon (the bold stripes of her trademark hat boxes can be seen to the left), there is a playful and dramatic atmosphere in her apartment. Two of the milliner's hats are displayed in one of the bedrooms (above). Strong, positive colours have been used throughout, and by the keeping walls bare and the furniture to a minimum, additions like the two chandeliers in the hallway (opposite) are fitting without being ostentatious.

When Anna Bonde and her family bought this old stone farmhouse in Provence thirteen years ago, 'It had nothing,' she recalls. 'There was not even a loo, no heating, nothing.' At the time she was working for an estate agents in the area and when this house came onto her books, she took her three children along to see it. 'They said to me, straightaway, if you don't buy this house we'll never come and see you again. So I had to!'

Anna had planned to use the farmhouse as a place to come in the summer months – a holiday home which they would do up gradually, as and when they could afford it. 'But it didn't go exactly according to plan,' she says. 'We came out for that first summer, and we never left.'

As much as the old stone walls of the property, its surroundings, including spectacular views of the mountains and a magnificent 300-year-old oak tree in the grounds, proved irresistible. Unforeseen as their move was, however, they didn't sell their other house for another seven years.

'We lived like spartans for a while, making something from nothing. This is when one's imagination can help. What's the saying? "Necessity is the mother of invention." Well, I'm the grandmother.'

Anna went to art school in Sweden, became a silver designer and later turned her interest to old textiles.

She amassed a considerable collection of antique French and Swedish fabrics, which she then transformed to accompany a line of iron furniture of her own design. Meanwhile, with her daughter, Ebba, she opened the French branch of the Swedish textile company Linum.

Examples of her work are found throughout the house: 'I always wanted a four-poster bed, but couldn't find one I liked, so I made one.' The result – a simple square of iron rods suspended from the ceiling over the bed – is not just elegant, but unique.

Although they were already happily living in a large house nearby, Anna and her family found they couldn't leave after spending just one summer here. Seven years later, after they had sold their original house, they added a spacious extension with a vast sliding glass wall (opposite) – but other luxuries in the house such as the Bruno Mathsson chaise longue, which came from a flea market, have been cleverly sourced or homemade.

anna bonde and arne tengblad

14

The little square, stone house, very typical of this region, now comprises three bedrooms, two studio spaces and two bathrooms. Once the family finally sold the other property they began building a new wing, with a large living room and another bedroom. An outhouse has been converted to make a dining room.

The new wing, with its sliding glass doors that disappear into the old stone structure, opens out into the garden. It couldn't be more different from the existing building. Elsewhere in the house Anna and Arne have kept the original tiled floors, old stone walls and exposed beams, but the new quarters are unrelentingly modern, even down to the wall-to-wall carpets. 'We didn't always agree on everything when we were deciding what we wanted,' says Anna, 'but we built it together. It took a long time.'

Arne is a sculptor and a painter, and his art – like Anna's furniture and textiles – is everywhere in the house, as are the couple's books. Arne, in particular, owns a vast collection of art books. Both have studios downstairs.

Anna has had the most input in the way the interior has been decorated (the colour scheme evolved, for example, as a result of her textile collection, which includes shades

Arne's paintings and sculptures can be seen here in the extension (above and right). Anna designed the iron sofa (opposite), with cushions covered in Swedish fabrics made by Linum. The coffee table is also one of her designs, iron legs have been added to an old oak door.

Anna has displayed a small, but
beautiful strip of vintage wallpaper by
simply hanging it onto a cupboard door
in the main bedroom. The decorative
feature above the bedroom door itself
was another lucky find from an antiques
market.

Anna made her four-poster bed (top left). A simple square of iron rods is suspended from the ceiling with curtains made from old linen sheets. The two spare bedrooms (above and right) see Linum curtains set against the traditional décor.

of blue and beige, Swedish and Provençal colours). She admits that she is often invited to take on interior design projects for friends and visitors who want to emulate her 'look' in their own homes.

'I always have to say no,' she says. 'I can't do this for someone else – it takes me years to do it just in my own house. And to make it like this I have to work with what I have. You can't fake it. Interior decoration is too personal. It's not about looking left and right at what's in fashion. I hate that. Interior design is about personal style, and that's timeless. At the moment, for example, everyone in France is having stainless steel kitchens fitted, which are so elegant but they'll be out of fashion in a few years time.'

a writer's palace in palma

On a street corner opposite Palma cathedral (above), Sebastian's house looks austere from the outside, just a modest gate, beyond which there is a courtyard and some steps that lead up to the first floor. Even if the gate is open and you can glimpse into the courtyard, you would never guess how large this palace is inside. The study (right and opposite) where Sebastian sometimes sits and writes is on the first floor. Like most of the rooms in the house, this one has only a couple of items of furniture arranged in the vast space, but all the rooms are piled high with books.

Within the 18th-century walls of Palma, the historic quarter of Mallorca's capital city, are many ancient churches, palaces and stately mansions, architectural souvenirs of its prosperous past. Not least, of course, the cathedral of Palma, la Seu, which enjoys a particularly spectacular location on the shore of the bay and fishing port.

Any visitors approaching Palma by sea cannot help but be impressed by its graceful architecture as it gradually emerges into view behind a shield of palm trees and colourful fishing boats.

La Seu was built on the site of a mosque. As legend would have it, one night in 1229, as Jaime I was on his way to recapture Mallorca, his fleet was struck by a terrible storm. He vowed to the Virgin Mary that if he survived nature's fury he would erect a church in her honour. And when, after the storm had blown over, he emerged safe and unharmed, he immediately set to work to fulfil his promise. Construction began in 1230 and the cathedral was finished in 1601.

Right behind this elegant Gothic temple, on the oldest street in the city, is the palace that Sebastian Camps calls home. It is so close to the cathedral that from his roof terrace you feel you might just be able to reach out and touch it.

Sebastian, a writer, curator and intellectual, lives here alone and plays the romantic role of 'writer in residence' in the palace. Such a site, overflowing with history, mystery and intrigue, is an astonishing place to be based and the privileged and dramatic surroundings suit him well. 'It is built on ruins,' he says. 'I fantasize all the time about discovering the last relics of the Romans!'

The palace has been in his family since the 1980s and Sebastian uses it as an urban 'pied à terre', spending weekdays here and weekends in the country. His parents

building across a courtyard houses so many rooms. Even Sebastian himself can't be very specific about how many there actually are, as the layout of each of the three floors sees the rooms flowing into one another, many of the large spaces have several doors and corridors are so spacious they constitute rooms in their own right too.

'I just see it as a whole house', he says, 'with four walls. It's just a place where you sleep.'

The previous owners had done little to the house during their time there. 'They were terrified that the whole house would crumble because there was a lot of damage to the roof,' explains Sebastian. But apart from fixing that, when the family bought it they left the house just as they found it. 'We did nothing – we just mended the fundamental things, like the roof, and that's all.'

In the huge, first-floor drawing room (opposite), the hexagonal tiles are the oldest in the house. The second floor, the planta noble (left and below), is one of Sebastian's favourite places to work. The palace can be difficult to heat in winter, so the writer creates a cosy camp by the fireside with his thermos to hand and often stays up working through the night.

live just a short drive away on their farm. Sebastian describes the palace as being 'quite big for Mallorca', and explains that he takes on much of the responsibility for the running of it.

The farm allows the family to be largely self sufficient – they grow all kinds of vegetables, almonds, olives and figs, while chickens keep fresh eggs in good supply. Sebastian visits often – typically returning to the palace after a large Sunday lunch laden with enough produce to see him through the rest of the week in the city.

Having been brought up in the countryside, Sebastian has more affinity with the rural way of life, its closeness to the land and to nature. This may explain why the palace, despite its extravagant size and grand proportions, has a refreshingly down to earth and unpretentious air.

'I am not someone who really belongs in the town,' Sebastian explains. 'But there is a poetical justice in our buying this house all those years ago – it is now finally in the hands of the people who live on the land.'

Accessed from a modest gate on a typically narrow old street, passers by would certainly never guess that this

There are many layers of history in the palace – the top floors, says Sebastian, were probably added some centuries later. 'And then you can discover a lot of 19th-century aesthetic snobbery – when they covered the beams with plaster ceilings and painted the doors, hiding all the original features.'

The beautiful tiled floors in every room meanwhile date from different periods: 'The hexagonal tiles you can see on the first floor are the oldest, for example. Then the others with the different patterns – which you can see in many other houses and apartments in Mallorca – are probably from the early 20th century.'

It has been a conscious decision on Sebastian's part not to make large design gestures or tamper with the fabric of the building in any way. 'I have a lot of artist friends and associates, architects and interior designers, who come here and say what they would do to the house. But I am very sceptical of all that – your home just becomes a show home – just for showing off and impressing people, although, of course, it isn't always that unambiguous. I would rather live in a way that keeps the spirit of the house alive.'

'I think my work as an art curator also makes me more respectful of the stains of time,' he continues. 'And of the hands that people have had in shaping it – and I mean "people" – not just artists.'

With its high ceilings, its tall, elegant doors and windows, in abundance, the atmosphere in the palace comes as much from the dramatic fall of light and shadows as it does from the furniture. There is not much furniture anyway, just some large, inherited pieces.

The books, meanwhile, are another matter: piled on every available surface, be it chair, mantelpiece, table, stair, or simply towering up from the beautiful tiled floors, Sebastian is constantly acquiring them. And new or second-hand, they have become almost part of the furniture. There may be a notable lack of bookshelves to store them on, but there is certainly no shortage of space.

People often have a very personal relationship with their books and Sebastian is no exception. He is especially philosophical about them: 'Right now books are the pillars of friendship,' he says. 'There is a continuum between reading and writing. Also this endless quantity of printed matter, of frozen voices, means continuity.'

Books, for Sebastian, give life to the house itself. 'The beauty of the house, in this sense? It's reading a Borges poem, a Proust paragraph, à voix haute, in a certain, filtered afternoon light.'

Be they Proust or Borges or otherwise, with its dramatic oversized rooms only serving to enhance rather than obliterate all the most intricate of details within them, the palace is certainly an appropriate home for such texts.

The tiled kitchen (opposite and below), on the first floor, has been kept authentic and fairly basic, with not much more than a sink, a stove and a small table. The door to the left of the table opens out onto a balcony over the courtyard.

This bedroom on the planta noble (above) has the same floor tiles as the study next door. One of the bedrooms (opposite) on the next floor up. Beyond this, there is just one more level – the roof terrace – which offers spectacular views of the cathedral next door, particularly at night when it is dramatically lit.

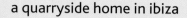
a quarryside home in ibiza

Composed of three separate buildings, this house has an unusual layout and also benefits from two spaces to sit and contemplate the stunning views over the valley. A terrace next to the main house (above) is a luxuriously green place to enjoy a meal in the shade. The outdoor kitchen in the top house (opposite), meanwhile, has an altogether different feel. The chairs have covers made from heavy-duty bright white cotton.

The pristine, white furnishings and cobalt blue paint that surrounds doorways and windows of this house immediately tell of its Mediterranean location. But deep in the woods, overlooking a sunny green valley, there are no other houses in sight and no clue at all that this might in fact be Ibiza.

An island renowned for its nightlife and clubbing scene, this house is absolute proof of another, infinitely more remote, relaxing side to the island. This Ibiza home is, however, far from typical.

Antique dealer and interior designer Béatrice Courmont and her partner Pierre, both Belgian, have lived here since the late 1970s. Pierre was already living on the island when they found this place – then a ruin – and Béatrice decided to leave her job as a fashion designer in Brussels and move here.

Their fascination with the property provided the impetus for the couple to spend the next twenty years renovating it. Transforming it, little by little, into the beautiful home they intend to live in for years to come, they have completed almost all of the work themselves.

Nestled in calm privacy amongst a pinewood in the centre of the island, the house is adjacent to a long-abandoned quarry and has spectacular views over the surrounding countryside and its mountainous backdrop. The property consists of three separate buildings, which were originally constructed to contain the generator and other such installations for the quarry.

Besides adapting, converting and extending the buildings to their needs, the work has included adding two bathrooms and – equally essential in Ibiza – a large swimming pool. Without the benefit of an architect, and in spurts depending on what funds would allow, over the years Béatrice and Pierre have forged a living space that is at once not only a comfortable, subtle place to be, but also uplifting and inspiring.

The house exudes a feeling of luxury. But, says Béatrice, this does not come from having filled it with designer objects or expensive textiles. 'There's hardly any expensive furniture at all here,' she says. 'This helps people who come here to feel comfortable – visitors always find the house charming, original and simple. Instead the luxury comes from the lifestyle that the house encourages – and from the surroundings: the view, the swimming pool, the space and the quietness.'

The garden, which Béatrice describes as 'romantic', wraps around the main house. Filled with fruit trees, shady mimosas and bright flowers, it joins the three buildings and feels as much like a room, a lively, functional, crucial part of the house, as any of the interior spaces.

Throughout all three buildings, the furnishings are consistently minimal and unpretentious. 'All the furniture and objects in the house come from flea markets on the island,' says Béatrice. 'We've collected what we needed as we've found bits and pieces we liked over the years – some was also brought over from Belgium when we first came. This is what makes the house warm, what we think makes it personal. Although

In the middle house, built into the side of the cliff, the rock is part of the construction and forms a feature that reminds the occupants of the bedroom just how deep in the Ibiza countryside they are (near right). The indoor kitchen in the main house (far right) opens out onto the living area (opposite), which in turn looks through one of the many boldly blue, framed doors towards a small office and bedroom (below).

we didn't always necessarily have much choice at the time, we are very happy with the way the house has turned out.'

One striking theme in the house is the heavy, white cotton fabric that covers almost all of the chairs. The opposite of impractical – a view many people have of white furnishings – Béatrice made the covers precisely because they would be so easy to wash. The white circles of the fabric draped over lampshades also help to diffuse the light, creating a more soothing effect. The uppermost building, which contains an outdoor kitchen and dining area, and one small bedroom, has a white curtain that runs across the open wall, protecting any diners from low sun.

Ultimately, the sense of calm and privacy that enfolds the house is exaggerated by the simple, unpretentious and comfortable atmosphere that Béatrice's eye for design and decoration has created. The benefits of the beautiful location are apparent throughout, but every room in the house has its own unique character. And every person who spends time there has their own favourite. Pierre, for example, favours the white, minimalist, restful room in the annex. Béatrice's grandchildren, meanwhile, love to create their own

play-houses, either in the quarry or in the upstairs studio, which is a little way from the main house.

The middle building is the smallest of the three and contains a bedroom and a bathroom, and a striking architectural quirk – built into the side of the cliff, part of the rock has been left to jut into the bedroom, the walls simply close around it.

The main living area is the lowest building of the three. Here, Béatrice's favourite room is a small, covered terrace that faces the swimming pool. She explains that it is the best place to spend the siesta hours, perhaps on one of the sofas surrounded by the many lush plants, or to offer guests an aperitif before dinner. For the same reasons – the sheer pleasure of relaxing, reclined amongst greenery and water – the smallest bathroom is arranged with a view onto the garden.

Besides the greenery, which pervades the house due to Béatrice's love of plants, colour is kept to a minimum. It makes the blue paintwork all the more dramatic. Setting off the pale ochre and white walls and unvarnished, unpainted or stripped wooden furniture, it creates a striking vibrancy to the house in a way that still seems to be natural and organic.

At 23 x 30 ft (7m x 9m), the kitchen is one of the largest and most distinctive rooms. Split over several levels, the room has both living and dining areas. The room is painted, and it is here that a liberal hand with the bold blue paintwork has really come into its own, instantly adding warmth and life to the space. Neutral, ochre tones contrast with doors and windows accented with the essential broad blue frames found throughout each building.

The rooms in all three buildings are decorated in the same colours and fabrics: mainly white textiles and neutral pale peach and ochre shades that sit unobtrusively with the stripped wooden doors and the furniture. The effect throughout is calming and warm, especially in the bedroom (right) and bathroom (left) in the lowest house of the three, where the family spend most of their time.

grand simplicity in belgravia

The large kitchen, which leads off to a courtyard on the left, is right in the centre of the apartment, with all the other rooms arranged around it. One of Maureen's many sinks (above), this one is in the 'washing up room', used for washing dishes. For washing food there is an old artist's sink in the kitchen (right). Next to the sink, the green vegetable rack, which Maureen found in a flea market, is an old trolley from a factory. 'I knew it was perfect for storing vegetables straightaway,' she says.

Situated in London's Belgravia, Maureen Doherty's home, although a basement apartment, is light, bright, clean and warm. It takes a huge leap of imagination to picture it in the state it was in when she bought it.

Returning from a few years spent living in Paris in the mid-1990s, Maureen opened Egg Trading, a shop and gallery on Kinnerton Street, and rented a flat above it with her young daughter, Jessica. Wanting to buy, she found that the property market had boomed during her time away and there was not much on offer that met her requirements. 'I needed to be near both my daughter and work at the time. My budget did not enable me to live above ground level in Belgravia,' she says. 'The agents laughed when I told them how much I had to spend! Finally, though, I found this space and I knew immediately that it would be fine. There was a lot of potential light, and it was near enough to walk to work and school, but no one else wanted it.'

The flat, on the lower floor of a Georgian house, is a large space and in a very desirable location, but other buyers had been put off because its previous occupants had been prostitutes: 'The walls were black and grey, and there were neon lights everywhere, it was filthy,' recalls Maureen. 'But I just took everything out and painted it white.'

maureen doherty

■

Maureen's study (opposite) is also a place where she can sit and relax and overlooks one of the two courtyards. String, like the examples in this basket, is one of the many 'everyday things' she loves to collect. She picks it up all over the world and uses it to wrap presents or to make labels for the items in her shop. In front of the kitchen window (above) Maureen displays some of the other useful, but beautiful, things she has collected – often ceramics, which she studied herself for six years while in Paris.

It was, in fact, a relatively simple process of stripping out what was there and letting some light in. The real work began only when Maureen embarked on a major overhaul of the space in 2002, moving the rooms, knocking down walls, and installing underfloor heating.

Originally, the basement would have been the servant's quarters where they cooked, did the laundry and stored the coal. The four caves where they kept the coal were 1000 sq ft (92 sq m) in area; Maureen has converted this space into a laundry room, a steam room, her study and a small single bedroom which she likes to call 'the Grade 8 room' or the 'vagrant's room' – this is where she used to put Jessica's boyfriends when they came to stay in her teenage years. In the centre is a large kitchen and leading off either side is Maureen's bedroom, bathroom and study, and 'the hock', Jessica's bedroom, bathroom and study, although she now lives in Paris.

Perhaps the most unusual thing about the apartment is that there is no sitting room, says Maureen. 'I hate them…they remind me of small talk. I always have conversations in gardens, in bed or most importantly around the kitchen table.'

Maureen previously worked in the fashion industry, but – just as Egg Trading is 'a shop for people who don't like to shop, for people who love clothes but are bored by fashion' – she is also entirely indifferent to trends or fads in her home. Resisting change for the sake of it and surrounding herself with things she loves and will always love, her style is original, ageless and timeless.

She doesn't believe, either, in using interior designers or architects when making a home – 'when they try to tell me what I should do here, or in the shop, it's like "get out the garlic!" – one's house should always represent one's personality, it needs to give you pleasure for the right reasons, because you love it and it's comfortable, not because it's fashionable.'

Maureen has succeeded in making the apartment look as if it hasn't been decorated. 'A lot of people come down here and they think they are in Barcelona or somewhere. They'll say things like, "That's clever how you left that bit as it was", and so on, but actually I haven't really left anything!'

When pushed, she describes her attitude to decoration as celebrating simplicity, light, fire and water: 'All the elements I love. All I've tried to do here is to bring light into the space. And water. There are seven sinks in the apartment, I am infatuated with water.'

Maureen's bedroom and bathroom
(opposite) are kept tidy and simple.
'I am always clearing and editing.
I dream of living as simply as possible
but never quite achieve it,' she says.
A large screen in classical stripes
(opposite, above, right) stands next
to the bed and hides her wardrobe. Most
of the furniture in the apartment was
bought in flea markets, or from
Christopher Howe, Maureen's favourite
antique dealer in Pimlico.

The wide, bright entrance hall (above),
like the rest of the apartment, is painted
white. 'Colour is impossible for me to live
with all the time in the city. If I had
houses in the country or another
continent I would possibly use colour,'
says Maureen. A glass door (above, right)
leads from the entrance hall into a steam
room, where some of the beautiful stones
Maureen has found and brought back
from various beaches are displayed
(right). 'Everything in my house is there
because it pleases me,' she says. 'Even
the stones – rocks please me.'

Roberto and Karin's desire to exalt the play of light and shadows on the walls means that they have been largely left bare, but there are a few exceptions: hanging along the back wall of Roberto's office are his own ink drawings of landscapes (right). A view of one of the bedrooms (below), with one of many old doors that Roberto has found and refurbished to be in keeping with the rest of the house. In the summer the grape arbour (above) just outside the kitchen gives protection from the sun's rays when dining outside.

Roberto and Karin Einaudi, an architect and art historian respectively, visit their farmhouse at Chiantennano (near Pienza, between Montepulciano and Siena) to regenerate themselves after the pressures of everyday professional life. When they return to work in Rome, it is with clear heads, fresh insights and with extra virgin olive oil, vegetables and fruit, all organically produced on their land.

The Einaudis wanted a house that was sufficiently large to accommodate themselves, their children and grandchildren, and those of their friends, and was near enough to Rome to visit every weekend. It was important, too, that it was in a beautiful, unspoilt area of historical

and paesaggistic value. After a year of systematically combing the countryside, they found it.

It was a ruin – overgrown with ivy and with the roof collapsed in many places, the house was ready to crumble into pieces. It needed major restoration. Together, the Einaudis took on the formidable task, redoing the roof (maintaining the existing old wooden rafters wherever possible and adding 'new' beams reclaimed from other old buildings where necessary), consolidating the walls and putting in new cotto floors on the ground floor, while restoring the existing ones on the upper floor.

'The first historical information we have relating to the building refers to its acquisition by the nearby benedictine monastery of Monteoliveto Maggiore in 1399, so its construction precedes that date,' explains Roberto. 'Originally, it may have been an outlook tower or a stop post along one of the many minor pilgrimage routes to Rome, judging from the exceptionally thick walls in the central part and its location on an ancient road along a crest. Over the centuries, it was enlarged by bits and pieces, giving it its characteristically articulated form, adapted to meet varying needs, typical of many of the rural farmhouses of southern Tuscany.'

During recent centuries several share cropper families working for an absentee landowner lived here. Traditionally, they occupied the upper floor, with the ground level used to house the animals and for the storage of produce.

The Einaudis use only part of the ground floor to store produce and tools, while the majority is common living spaces, including a large kitchen–dining room, a living room, two studio spaces and a small bathroom. A new internal staircase leads up to five bedrooms and a large living room complete with its original fireplace and oven. Two simple bathrooms have also been added to the first floor.

Throughout the restructuring and renovation, the Einaudis' main aim was to preserve the original character of the building and its surroundings.

'It was important to respect what our predecessors had made of the place. That meant choosing materials and workmanship that corresponded as closely as possible to the building's history.'

It wasn't always easy: reinforcing crumbling walls, without loosing the character they had acquired over the centuries, and introducing such elements of modern life as toilets and heating in a harmonious way all presented particular challenges. 'I had to instruct the contractor how to keep and sustain the

A large fireplace in what used to be the stables, now the living room (opposite), was constructed from reclaimed bricks and wooden beams. The room is heated by air passing behind the fire and coming in through a series of openings on the mantlepiece. A new cotto floor replaces the old one damaged beyond repair, but maintains the memory of the V-shaped gutter originally in the stable. On display around the house, unusual arrangements of oak branches and roses are testimony to Karin's expert skills with nature. The entrance hall to the upper level (below), in one of the oldest parts of the house, boasts the original cotto floor, fireplace and oven.

falling ancient walls rather than tear them down and rebuild them, which to him would have been far simpler,' recalls Roberto. 'To stucco the walls, I told the workmen they had to forget the modern techniques they had learned in order to bring out their innate characteristics and make them vibrate with reflected light.'

Two large fireplaces in what used to be the stables were constructed from reclaimed bricks and wooden beams. Air, filtered from outside, goes under the floor and is heated as it passes behind the fire, entering the room through a series of openings on the mantlepiece.

The intensive nature of the work is only one reason why the interior design and decoration has been limited in the house. 'I have an innate dislike for the word "decoration" when applied to architecture, colour and furnishings,' says Roberto. 'I feel that the character of a place must come not from a desire to "decorate", but the need to discover and exalt the intimate nature of the space. Here the colours, textures and forms all come from the materials available, the play of light on the surfaces and the juxtaposition of forms and their functions.'

Their iconoclastic attitudes mean the walls have been largely left bare, but there are a few exceptions: Roberto's ink drawings of landscapes are hung up the staircase, while paintings by the architect's mother add life to the corridor on the first floor.

Most of the furniture was acquired from a local secondhand dealer who could provide pieces of original, rustic furniture that would look at home. Other pieces, such as the piano, were brought from Rome. A kitchen bench was made by a stone cutter out of local limestone, as was the garden dining table under the grape arbour.

Set in the idyllic landscape of Chiantennano, the house lies on a slope between the Einaudis' olive grove and a cypress alley, and it has panoramic views of fields, forests and ancient hill towns, with the rounded silhouette of Monte Amiata dominating the horizon.

When asked what they like most about the house, the Einaudis respond that paradoxically it is not the house itself, but its relationship to its surroundings.

'Each season has its appropriate indoor–outdoor relationship,' says Roberto. 'In the winter, even in January, we can eat outside in the entry court where the sun is collected and trapped to form a comfortable space. In the summer the grape arbour gives protection from the sun's rays. At the back of the house, as an extension to the living room, the court is paved with the bricks reclaimed from the stables, covered with wisteria and rose arbours. It is a wonderful place to lounge and eat in the summer.'

The window in the large spare bedroom looks out over the valley (opposite). The views from the house, which lies on a slope between an olive grove and a cypress alley, are one of the things that keeps the couple returning here to regenerate themselves after their busy lives in Rome. Some of the doors in the house are original, but where they were missing, or beyond repair, Roberto carefully sourced others from the area that would be in keeping (below).

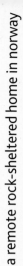

This remote house is sandwiched between the sea and a steep cliff, and the only neighbours for miles are sheep. It is protected from the frequent violent storms and the wind by a large rock (above). Tulla and Terje have done as little as possible to the space, preferring to preserve and refurbish what was there already. Downstairs (above, right) they installed an old iron stove and the living room (below) is decorated with original artwork. Upstairs in the bedroom (opposite) they discovered that the walls were covered with old sails, painted as if they were wallpaper. The sails would have been put up to give further shelter from the extreme weather to which the sea-facing side of the house is exposed.

Discovering Lofoten while teaching at an art school there, Tulla Elieson, a ceramist, and Terje Ressell, a painter, found what is now their summerhouse, a small, isolated, 18th-century timber building, 'hiding' behind a huge rock. Although happily settled in the south-east of Norway, the pair decided to rescue the house, which had been forgotten by the rest of Lofoten and left empty for more than forty years. Eventually tracking down its owner, they bought it and embarked on its restoration.

Lofoten is a hectic centre of cod fishing in the winter and, with twenty-four hours of daylight in the summer, it is one of the best spots to contemplate the midnight sun which occurs because at midnight the sun is over the sea towards the north and at noon it is over the large mountain to the south. Exposed to the violent south-west wind, however, the house was built next to the rock for protection.

Tulla and Terje discovered old painted sails lining the walls of the north-facing bedroom upstairs. Intended to provide further shelter from the wind, they are now one of Tulla's best-loved features: 'If the house hadn't been empty all those years they would have been removed long ago.' While making it a comfortable place to live, they also strove to preserve the house's history. As well as the sails there are other quirks which give the interior intense character: 'The people who lived here were poor, timber was expensive as it was scarce,' explains Tulla. 'They used local materials as much as possible; sand and stone, bound together with concrete. Cracks between the timber logs were filled in with moss and old fishing net.'

A classical old Lofot house, comprising a kitchen, a living room and four bedrooms, 'It sits on a site which contained just enough grass to sustain a family of ten, living from fishing, some sheep, a cow or two, and some

The living room (left), painted in warm earthy tones and decorated with an eclectic mix of different fabrics and colours, is perfect for thawing out on a stormy day. With no running water (Tulla and Terje collect it from a nearby mountain stream) and difficult access (the nearest road is over a mile away), a comfortable, if simple, place to relax is essential.

From the kitchen windows (right) Norway's famous midnight sun can be seen, over the sea. A collection of different wooden chairs surround the vast kitchen table, which the couple found in a second-hand shop after spending a long time looking for something that would be authentically distressed enough for the space.

potato cultivation. They also burned seaweed to produce jod for sale.'

As it contained no furniture when Tulla and Terje bought the house, sourcing items faithful to its history as a poor family home was a difficult task. 'It shouldn't be in any way posh or trendy, so we couldn't buy antiques,' says Tulla. 'We ended up using the equipment from our own first flat as poor artists.'

An example of their approach is the kitchen table. Bought in an ordinary second-hand shop, its painted surface is covered in scars from having been a working surface for more than a century. 'We had been looking for one as unpretentious as this for a long time,' she laughs.

As someone who is particularly conscious of the environment, Pedro likes to keep his own impact on it as small as he can, which means, among other things, not taking up too much space. Even though his beach house (above) is newer than the others in this small collection of buildings, his way of life here is traditional. The house consists of one main open space (opposite), containing the living and dining rooms and the kitchen – though most of the living here takes place outside. Pedro has constructed a small sink from old stone and a collection of reclaimed tiles (opposite, below, right).

Pedro Espirito Santo, an interior designer, strongly believes that one should never interfere with nature unless it is strictly necessary. Working and living between Portugal and Brazil, he has a flat and an office in Lisbon, but he spends as much time as he can at his beach house in Alentejo in the south of Portugal, a place he describes as 'the last wild place in Europe. Even in August.'

The house is so small and basic that Pedro's idea of a living room is the shady patch underneath the huge pine trees outside, yet it is exactly for these reasons that for those who visit, the place is in fact the height of luxury – the ultimate getaway, close to the beach and in an extremely amenable climate.

One of a group of similar, small buildings, the houses were all originally constructed for the labourers who worked in Alentejo's thousands of acres of forests nearby.

Pedro, along with two of his cousins, Louise and Martin, bought up several properties here at the end of the 1980s. 'I fell in love with the area, with the house and the lifestyle of the people here,' he recalls. 'It is a place where you can feel completely free.'

This feeling of freedom may have something to do with the beautiful stretch of Atlantic coast near the house. But beyond that, says Pedro, it is because he has been able to keep everything inside simple, authentic and straightforward.

'As an interior designer, I have lived in some fantastic houses,' he explains. 'Few people can understand this evolution – that I would come here – because it is the opposite way of living, the opposite to design and decoration. But in these little houses everything is so simple, it's the essence of life.'

The interior is both practically and aesthetically well organized. Pedro, who is very ecologically aware, offsets his frequent fuel-guzzling flights to Brazil by avoiding excessive consumption and consumerism in other areas of his life. Preferring to recycle, reuse or reappropriate where he can, he has sourced much of the furniture for this house second hand. Generally this has meant trading items with friends who no longer had any use for something themselves, or finding pieces in the local (so-called) junk shop. One man's trash is another man's treasure, and especially when you've such a good eye

The kitchen space (above) is divided from the living area by a low wall. Pedro, a designer, has created an attractive still-life arrangement from a mixture of worn objects. The bedroom (opposite), like the rest of the building, is painted white to keep it cool.

for it: sometimes he just comes across exactly what he's looking for on the street, he says.

Ultimately, however, the furnishings in the house are minimal – just the bare necessities for him and his guests. There is a small dining table, a mattress with some colourful cushions, a kitchen, storage basics and very little else.

The kitchen and dining room are arranged as one open space, which also works as a cosy indoor living room. The deck outside, however, furnished with hammocks and wooden chairs, is the real living area, and where Pedro can be found most of the time. The bedroom and the shower are self contained, leading off from the main room.

Decoration, too, is kept basic though never to the point of being austere. Pedro has freely mixed textiles, styles and colours throughout – the walls are white, the doors are brightly painted in different shades, while multi-coloured cushions, curtains and rugs – usually striped – can be seen everywhere. 'I'm not worried about the

"rules" of good taste,' says the designer. 'I don't care about fashion in this house, I just try to keep it all simple and down to earth.'

The houses have all been carefully kept in the same state as when they were first built, there is no air conditioning or heating, and in the winter wood fires provide all the extra warmth needed in this hot climate. Pedro's essential 'comforts' here are the luxuries of electricity, water and 'good beds'.

Forming a close, neighbourly community where outdoor life takes precedence, Pedro spends much of his time socializing, whether the cousins are all here at once, or whether guests take up residence here instead. Though he entertains a great deal, 'because people love it so much they want to come here all the time,' he always finds the space and time in the house simply to be. 'To always be busy and doing things is very easy,' he reflects. 'To stop is very difficult. Here, I always can.'

The completely white background means that Pedro does not have to be precious about coordinating colours and fabrics, although simple stripes feature everywhere, usually in bright colours. The decoration is likely to have been much the same when the houses were first built, with a free mix of colours, textiles and styles, and brightly painted doors and ragrugs on the floor.

A large fireplace (right) is rarely used thanks to the hot climate, but provides a useful shelf for collections of bright ornaments and candles. Pedro found most of the furniture and kitchen equipment (below) in local thrift shops, even down to the mismatching tiles used to line the bottom of the shower (below, right). The entrance from the 'living room' outside is always open to friends and family, something that is key to Pedro's very sociable way of living.

In Victor's apartment in the old quarter of the town, the bedroom balcony (above, left) looks out over a typical street. It is furnished with little more than the essential bed and chair, although to Victor the inclusion of art is just as important. The large photograph seen here is by Spanish photographer Charles Conconst (above, right). A large terrace at the back of the apartment (right) faces the ancient city wall. Reflected floodlights from the wall create stunningly atmospheric lighting on the terrace after sundown.

Victor Esposito believes that in a way he must have been destined to live in this apartment. On the top floor of an old building right next to the old city walls in Ibiza, he moved here in 2002, after he had dreamt about it. 'In my dream I thought, "one day I am sure I will live there"', laughs Victor. 'And then I found out that a good friend of mine had a hairdressing salon on the ground floor of the same building. I asked him if he knew the owners of the building, he put me in touch, I went to see them and they sold me this apartment!'

Victor had moved to Ibiza many years before, buying and renovating small apartments in the old town, before selling them on. He had been living in the countryside himself, where he had bought and restored two old fincas – both now fine examples of his own light creative touch.

Although Victor is used to working with an architect and quite often finds himself undertaking considerable refurbishment works on apartments, this particular one, where he now lives and works the majority of the time, is an exception. 'I didn't touch anything,' he says. 'The floors are original and the kitchen is original. Everything is like it was when it was built. I just painted it white.'

The starting point – with its stunning tiled floors, attractive proportions and large windows – was

admittedly a good canvas. On the fourth floor of a 19th-century building (according to Victor's professional estimate it was built in around 1870), the apartment comprises a living room, two sitting rooms, a study, a bedroom, a kitchen and a bathroom. The latter has also been left pretty much in its original condition. The whole apartment is about 1600 sq ft (150 sq m).

Outdoor space includes a terrace at the back – large enough for a table and chairs – which is filled with plants, two balconies overlooking the street at the front and a roof terrace on the top of the building.

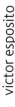

The long corridor (above, left) is furnished with a Balinese kayak that Victor found in a shop in Paris and opens onto a small sitting room (above, right). The balcony, like the one in the bedroom, overlooks the street.

The kitchen (right) has largely been left as Victor found it when he moved in and contains many of the original features (such as the tiles on the wall and the floor). Fitting in with his love of 20th-century vintage furniture, Victor has installed a modern, retro fridge. The bathroom (opposite), like the kitchen, has many of its original features intact, the only thing Victor needed to do to give it a contemporary feel was to paint the walls white.

The apartment was built right next to the ancient city wall, La Muralla, which provides an unusual view, and from the back terrace it is so close you can almost reach out and touch it. La Muralla, perhaps surprisingly, is in no way oppressive, nor does it block any of the apartment's light. In fact, at night when the wall is spectacularly floodlit, the back terrace and adjoining rooms are bathed in a beautiful reflected light that is wonderfully atmospheric. It is one of the things that Victor loves best about the apartment, plus, he says, it would be almost impossible to achieve using domestic lighting.

Victor himself is a creative, self-made citizen of the world: his parents are Italian, but he was born and brought up in France. His hometown before he moved to Ibiza was Marseille, and even while still in his early twenties, he was running a successful restaurant with an art gallery and cinema in the city. When he first moved to Ibiza Victor decided he wanted to try something different, and he opened a small interior design shop, where he sold furniture, textiles and accessories: all making up a very personal mix of things that appealed to his own taste and style, often including items that he had brought back from his numerous far-flung trips.

The special 'Victor touch' that made his shop so successful is very evident in this apartment where he now lives. Respecting the original elements such as the doors, tiles and fittings, the fresh coat of white paint combines with his eclectic mix of furniture to create a space that is light, comfortable and timeless. 'I like to mix styles,' he says, describing how he favours vintage 20th-century furniture above new pieces, 'from many different periods and places, but I especially like the shapes and colours of the 1970s.'

Victor picked up some pieces on his travels (not always the obvious acquisitions: the Balinese wooden kayak, for example, he bought in a shop in Paris). Otherwise much of the furniture in the apartment was bought from his friends Abi and Igor at a flea market in Marseille. Other pieces have come from another friend, the Iranian

architect Pascal Cheikh Djavadi, who designed the large sofa in the sitting room, for example; or are gifts: the cowskin rug on the sitting room floor is a souvenir from Argentina. Victor's creative friends are also largely responsible for the art on the walls: altogether he has amassed an impressive collection of contemporary photographic prints – from the abstract black-and-white shots by Antoine Le Grand on either side of the doors leading to the balcony; to a large image by Spanish photographer Charles Conconst in the bedroom.

Home, for Victor, is not a showcase for his considerable skills in refurbishment. It is absolutely where his heart is: 'It's important that the place where you live is like a dream,' he explains. 'It's crucial that it feels right when you open the door, and when you walk in you feel like you are living in your dream.'

The living room opens onto the terrace, while built-in cupboards (left) – original features of the apartment – house Victor's books and, here, an eclectic display of various artefacts. Victor collected chairs, often classic designs from the 1960s and 1970s, before it was fashionable to do so and today his mix of furniture in the apartment is enviable. The cowskin on the floor (opposite) was a gift from an Argentinian architect friend.

The Graff Nielsens' weekend home more closely resembles a country cottage than a houseboat (above). With two storeys and ample decking on both, it provides more than enough space for the family of four. One of several stone sculptures in the houseboat by Leo Andersen (above, right). The living area (opposite), at sea level, is decorated with blues, greys, browns and neutral sandy colours that reflect the surroundings, but the family wanted to avoid a nautical look.

There are very few houseboats in Denmark, and – surprisingly perhaps for a country surrounded by water – even fewer legal places to moor them. A matter of some contention between the Danish citizens and the politicians, it meant that when this houseboat was built in Hvide Sande, it was all over the news.

Hvide Sande Skibs & Baadebyggeri was a small, struggling shipyard that built and repaired boats, but they had an idea – they decided to rally against convention and established a new branch. Called Seasight, the new business was to be dedicated solely to building and developing houseboats and small, simple apartments. It took off almost immediately.

The small, close-knit community was very open to the idea of this alternative way of living. These houseboats were designed to be both homely and comfortable, but not 'hippyish' in any way.

The houseboat's developers gave the project a big media push during its conception. Several open-house weekends were held and people came from all over the country, including the Graff Nielsen family for whom it was love at first sight.

Michael Graff Nielsen, a businessman himself, had first heard of the project in its early stages and knew straightaway that he wanted to be involved. He bought the very first houseboat – a beautiful, blue, two-storey

often associated with. 'It's not always necessary to have furniture made especially for a boat, which many people seem to believe,' says Michael.

The furniture is evocative of a relaxed lifestyle: from the chaise longue on the first floor, to the large, solid oak dining table. The artwork, meanwhile, has a spiritual feel, chosen to fit in with the already calm surroundings.

The inspiration for the colour scheme, which is mainly composed of light blues and sandy browns, was taken from the houseboat's immediate natural environment. Materials, too, have been kept natural (solid wood floors, cotton and wool textiles, marble accessories) in an attempt to unite the look and feel between inside and outside. 'No plastic laminate, vinyl, acrylic or anything synthetic like that is used anywhere,' explains Michael.

With all the comforts of a conventional house, apart from the ever-changing views and the slight slant of the external walls, you wouldn't necessarily know you were on a boat at all. One gets a strong feeling of freedom and any preconceptions that life on a boat could be in any way limiting are left behind.

For all the attention that the new houseboats have received in the media, the area has avoided becoming a tourist trap. On the contrary, and this is especially the case with the Graff Nielsen family, it means a return to healthy, simple, seaside living.

A small dining room is separated from the kitchen by a low wall, maximizing the rooms' proportions (above). A Leo Andersen sculpture (below, right). Stairs lead up from the kitchen–dining area to the living room and the large deck (opposite). Natural materials used everywhere give an aura of tranquillity to the Graff Nielsens' life on the water, and besides the sloping walls and the view out of the windows you might not realize you were on a boat.

'cottage' – and now visits frequently with his wife Maj, a craft teacher, and his two children.

The family live two hours' drive towards the north east, but make time to visit the houseboat most weekends and for the holidays. The local fishermen who moor their own boats next door to the houseboat in its sheltered harbour have welcomed them into the community and always offer to bring them fresh fish in the evenings.

Somewhat belying its traditional, picturesque exterior, inside the houseboat is modern and functional. The overall style and the furniture are not too different from what you might see in a land-bound house – a deliberate decision, and a refreshing alternative to the clichéd nautical aesthetic that this type of residence is so

Living in an 18th-century Charentaise, restoration is central to Mathilde's work as a furniture designer and she is always able to see the beauty and potential in furniture and fixtures that others might discard as old or beyond use. Old support beams (above, right) are favoured over modern replacements inside and out. While many such houses in the region have been refurbished expensively by covering over features such as these old tiled floors in the entrance hall (opposite) and worn plasterwork on the walls, Mathilde's approach has been to strip it down to its original elements and look after what is left.

There is one thing that guests visiting Mathilde Labrouche's hideaway home almost always comment on – and it's not the picture-perfect scenery, the gorgeous original stone-tiled floors or the house's interesting antique fixtures, but their fantastic night's sleep. 'People sleep excessively well here,' says the interior designer. 'The whole world is rushing around – too many thoughts, too much stress. The idea of coming back to the essentials and respecting comfort and softness reminds people of feelings from their childhood and of simplicity.'

Mathilde 's house, an 18th-century Charentaise, is situated in Saintonge. 'It's the land of "songes", or dreams,' she explains, which is rather appropriate. The climate is sunny and the scenery, rolling hills and woods.

Mathilde was born and brought up in the village and has known the house since her childhood. 'It was just the same then as it is now,' she says. 'It was lived in by a farmer and his mother, and I used to buy eggs from old "mother Alice".'

Mathilde's family lived in a beautiful house next door and when the opportunity arose Mathilde's mother bought the house for her. It is an unusual but touching story: 'My mother's grandmother was once a servant

in the house so my mother buying it for me held special significance,' she explains.

These days, the house is often filled with children: Pablo and Rosa, Mathilde's children, and the children of her three brothers and two sisters – altogether she boasts seventeen nieces and nephews and four grand nieces and nephews – along with the children of various friends.

'And everybody has animals: donkeys, horses, chickens, dogs, cats, elephants,' she laughs. 'We, personally, have two fat cats, Billy the old one and Max the new one.' It is a full house, certainly.

In this part of the region, known as 'Haute Saintonge', there are a few similar houses, but by and large they have been restored without respect for their origins – something that is of utmost importance to Mathilde and has undoubtedly given this particular house such an extraordinarily peaceful ambience, despite the number of its inhabitants.

'I like this house because there have been no modifications since the 18th century; the floors, walls, attics and barns have been left untouched,' says Mathilde. 'My mother, too, was dedicated to preserving these old houses and the ambience particular to them, another reason why she bought this one.'

Having been an antique dealer for many years, Mathilde eventually began creating different pieces of furniture herself and became interested in interior design. She is well known throughout Europe for her furniture line created from antique, decorative architectural elements she finds and refashions.

Hunting down old materials such as doors, parts of flooring, pillars and balustrades, her use of materials is both distinctive and original. She made much of the furniture in the house specially — including all the beds — so they fit the space in a way that would never be possible with bought items.

As well as large pieces of furniture, Mathilde also recycles fabrics, porcelain and flooring, giving a new lease of life to the old, discarded and unwanted. Her talent is such that she can make an attractive lampshade by seemingly casually tossing an old piece of linen over a lampstand. What would appear messy in other houses, becomes artful and chic with her ability to see the beauty in the most unconventional and raw of materials.

But even for someone with professional expertise, however, bringing this particular Charentaise up to date

Sparse it may be, but Mathilde's minimalism is not without soul. Rather, she makes a feature of every item, however small. In the living room (opposite), which is large and open plan and contains several of Mathilde's own creations, a pair of baby's shoes are hanging above the fireplace, for example, while the prominent display of an old watering-can encourages a closer look. The ornamental pieces against the wall were once part of a carousel. One of Mathilde's lamps (below); a piece of cloth thrown over a lamp base becomes an object of beauty.

Achieving this meant that the materials had to be chosen very carefully and Mathilde had to be disciplined about keeping the number of objects and accessories to a bare minimum.

Doing so, which as many people who have tried and failed will know, is not as easy as it sounds, but Mathilde is very strict about keeping to her rules. 'The non accumulation of objects is essential for me,' she explains. 'Objects and colours should be in suspension; the air should flow around and encircle the rooms and the objects. I'm happy with the results, but it does demand daily rigour, housecleaning and flexibility to maintain it this way.'

One manifestation of this philosophy, and a crucial element in the workings of the house, is the bathroom. A little way from the main building in a small outhouse across the courtyard, 'It is very simple,' says Mathilde, 'and the sensation of being hidden by nature to wash oneself is very pleasant. All bodily hygiene happens outside here – and I think this is important for the balance and purification of the place.'

The decoration of the house may be minimal, but it is far from clinical or anonymous. Conversely, it is welcoming and wholesome, and a rich personality shines through the simplicity: 'I don't like lots of things. I like nothingness. This house is the philosophy of nothingness,' says Mathilde.

The children's drawings have held an important place in the decoration, while the furniture and objects all seem to have a story to tell. Her favourite item of furniture in the house is one of the few large additions that she did not actually make herself. Complementing her work perfectly, however, the beautifully painted cast-iron stove, which is installed in the large, open kitchen next to one of the house's grand fireplaces, is Mathilde's most treasured possession. A part of the history, the stove belonged to an elderly woman who lived in a little château nearby and was given to Mathilde as a Christmas present by her parents, who kept it hidden under a blanket.

In the kitchen (above) an old painted stove, a gift to Mathilde from her parents, takes pride of place next to one of the house's many large fireplaces. The designer salvages old architectural relics and recycles them into new features and furniture (opposite). A decorative door, here, forms a backdrop to the draining board, while another brings interest to the basin, creating a shelf at the same time.

without spoiling it in any way was never going to be easy. 'My challenge with the structure of the house was to bring modernity into it without shattering the aesthetic or erasing the patina of time,' she explains, and it was the same with the interior decoration. Although some walls have been painted, a great deal of it has been left as she found it.

The farmhouse certainly does not appear neglected (far from it) or unfinished, despite this approach, and the reason for this, according to Mathilde, is that she has been careful to keep everything as simple as possible. 'My aim was to place objects and furniture in such a way as to render them "invisible". My principal occupation has always been abstraction. I want to create abstract images with design.'

An old upholstered sofa (below) gives a rare splash of colour in one of the entrances to the house. Besides a few floral textiles and several bright green internal doors, the raw, natural materials everywhere mean the interior colour palette is a mix of ancient brown woods and warm, mottled off-whites. Looking through the living room doors (opposite) into the bedrooms beyond.

In this house the beauty is all in the details, especially the materials. The beds (left and opposite) were made by Mathilde herself from old wooden doors and architectural elements that she has salvaged from all over the Bordeaux region.

The bathroom (below) is housed in a small building, just across the courtyard. Although visiting it requires a trip outdoors, the idea was to separate the rituals of bodily hygiene from the main living area, while the surrounding greenery gives the sensation of 'being hidden in nature'.

The building's long evolution, continued by its current inhabitants, has resulted in a maze of intricate, complex spaces. A small street runs in through the large front gate (which Gustav built himself) and under the main house. It passes beneath three stone arches before wrapping around and rising behind the house. Including a pigeon tower and stables, the house has many unusual architectural features. The entrance (opposite), seen here with the drawing table and computer, is also the office. Conceding to the landscape, the ground floor undulates over many different levels; these steps lead up to the back of the house, towards the living room and kitchen.

Set on a hillside overlooking the Oppède Valley with Oppède le Vieux and the Lubéron Mountain in the background, 'Le Gougeas' is the Provençal home of Gustav and Ylva Langenskiold and their three children.

Built at the beginning of the 18th century, the building is rich in history – it is even said that the Marquis de Sade came here to take refuge when he was fleeing his château in nearby Lacoste. Stones on various walls of the building have dates etched into their surfaces. The year of the French Revolution, 1789, as well as other, earlier

dates inscribed bear testimony to the house's gradual construction and evolution as more space was required over time.

Once a farm, it now encompasses the surrounding buildings. At the beginning of the 20th century, an earthquake disturbed the grounds; the water table dropped and the nearby well was left redundant.

The house was then abandoned until the arrival of the Langenskiolds in 2001. The couple, who moved in with their eldest child and cat, Georges, were instantly attracted to the house.

'When we first saw it, Ylva said, "This is it",' recalls Gustav. 'I thought the same, but I also knew how much work was necessary.' As an architect working mainly on renovations and new-build private homes, Gustav was in a perfect position to take on the challenge. Having grown up in Provence, he was keen to return after his schooling at the Architectural Association and stint at David Chipperfield Architects in London. 'My whole family here have always been restoring houses; I know the local architecture quite well and felt that to set up a practice would be something I would feel comfortable with,' he says.

'When we left England, we only had an idea of the type of house we would have liked to find,' Gustav explains. Once they did, they lived with his parents for a year to enable them to do all the necessary work and moved in just before Elinor, their second child, was born.

'We had only done the bare essentials in order to move in and have kept on working on the house since then. It does not seem like we will ever get it finished. That is also one of our aims: to always be working on it.'

Le Gougeas's unusual features include a pigeon tower and a stable, as well as the arches in the entrance that Gustav and Ylva wanted to leave intact and this has prevented them altering the layout completely just to suit their family life better.

Most of the rooms were separated by thick walls or narrow staircases, too, but with a few small interventions they have reorganized the house so that the spaces connect logically.

The family's favourite room in the house is the kitchen, a light, high-ceilinged space that boasts a large, south-facing terrace, overlooking the valley with its olive groves and vineyards.

'We are very pleased with what we have achieved and we are very excited about what is still to be done. What we are proud of is that what first attracted us to the house is still here – we can still recognize the house as we first saw it. In fact, sometimes it feels like we haven't done much at all.'

'I think we were lucky to have found such an unspoilt house,' says Gustav on reflection. 'They have become very rare in this area. I am glad to think that having gone through this we have helped to renew this house without taking away the charm. While we've been dreaming of what it could become, throughout the whole process the reality of the work to be done has always kept our feet on the ground.'

Everyone in the family is artistic and practical, so it is not just a case of knowing what effect they want in the house, but also being able to make it themselves. Ylva visited local flea markets throughout the renovation period and found old doors and cupboards which she recycled inside the house. Gustav made the unusual and elegant thin window and door frames himself, while the cushions seen here (left) were made using Swedish textiles from Gustav's mother's Linum collection.

As a family home (left), it's not too serious and there is a preference for practicality over fashion. The children love it. Oscar, the eldest, says he used to wish they could all move to a newer, more modern house, but now is the first to admit that he loves it, 'even if there are more spiders.'

The luxuriously large kitchen (right) looks out onto a spacious terrace. Gustav, an architect, designed the kitchen units – in Fraque wood – and they were made by a local carpenter. He also designed and made the iron door frames that lead out onto the terrace. The original yellow Arne Jacobsen chairs, which surround the table, have been in the family for a long time and were brought over from Sweden.

Coats and boots are lined up – though tidily – in the main entrance to the house (right). The enormous original fireplace has been restored and is in regular use. The striped Swedish Linum textiles (below) have been put to good use, this time as a vast and elegant curtain over a wall of storage shelves. The door seen here leads from the living room to outside.

a church in the hudson valley

For jewelry designer Gabriella Kiss, working in a converted church, where the largest room can accommodate an 18-foot Christmas tree, can be somewhat overwhelming. But in every other respect it suits the family's lifestyle perfectly.

The hamlet, where Chris and Gabriella live in an old, converted, timber-clad church (above), consisting of 'a country store and post office, but without much more than that,' is in the picturesque Hudson Valley, surrounded by rolling hills and very little development. Traditionally, the area was known for its dairy farms, but today the number of farms has diminished and it has become much more residential. The largest room (opposite) has many uses.

Aside from being ideal for gatherings and basketball, it works excellently as a space for displaying modern and primitive design, which Gabriella and her husband Chris Lehrecke have been collecting for more than twenty years. Chris himself has been designing and building furniture for most of that period, too, and the space is filled with his pieces and those they have collected.

The converted Baptist church, in a pleasant hamlet about twenty miles from the Hudson River, is home to the couple, their two sons, Jack and Augie, and their two cats and two dogs. They first heard about it through a friend in New York: 'She knew the previous owner from her childhood,' explains Chris. 'He was a classical musician and used it as his weekend home for twenty years, restoring it and doing much of the original conversion.' Chris and Gabriella were looking to leave New York, where they had both developed a strong market for their work. 'Being two hours from the city, but not feeling suburban was appealing to the both of us,' he says.

When Chris and Gabriella moved in they continued the process: painting, organizing the lighting and re-doing the kitchen and the terrace behind the church. Built

in 1820 it is a typical New England church of this period in that the aesthetic is very sparse, almost Shaker in style. In its conversion into a home the front third of the church was transformed into a comfortable living space by extending the choir loft and building rooms underneath. There is also access to the bell tower via a spiral staircase. This part of the house has four separate bedroom areas and three bathrooms.

'The rear two-thirds of the church is wide open, pretty much exactly the way it was 100 years ago,' says Chris. Although they spend most of their time in the front of the church, the back is an incredibly beautiful space and works very well with Chris and Gabriella's spare and simple aesthetic, which includes a collection of artefacts and their own work.

The style and character of the old church is now defined at least as much by Chris's own elegant yet homey furniture as by its former use as a place of worship. His pieces, which demonstrate skilled craftsmanship using American wood indigenous to the area such as ash, maple, walnut, hickory and butternut wood, recall the graphic minimal lines of Japanese and Shaker design as well as the 1950s Scandinavian styles he now collects.

Gabriella, who likes to decorate in a smaller and more intimate way and has had to work harder at finding those places where she is able to do that here, resolved the difficulty by buying a small house across the street. 'She spent two years renovating it exquisitely into her jewel-like studio,' says Chris. But Gabriella's influence is not confined to her work space and the fine details of the natural phenomena – from slender branches to fossils and feathers – that inspire her jewelry are displayed everywhere. The overall effect is a harmonious balance of weight, scale and nature that make the church, though still vast, anything but intimidating.

Chris's elegant furniture can be seen throughout the house, including in the kitchen area (above and right), where it complements the old American cooking range.

The enormous main living space has multiple functions, including an office (opposite), a dining room, a living room and a children's play area. A mezzanine, which runs the entire length of the room, is a quiet place where the family go to sit and read.

Gabriella and Chris, a jewelry designer
and furniture designer respectively, both
take inspiration from the natural world.
While Gabriella's influences, displayed
around the house, tend to be more
intricate and delicate such as the
collection of corals (right), Chris's come
from the wood that he works with,
often the imperfections or quirks in the
material. His pedestals (below) are one
of his signature designs.

chris lehrecke and gabriella kiss

The quilt in the main bedroom (above, left and above, right) was brought back from Africa by a friend; the watercolour of a tree is by Mats Gustavson, one of the couple's many artist friends. The entrance hall (top right) is home to one of Chris's pedestals. The unusual shower curtain in the vast bathroom (opposite) was fabricated by the house's previous owner. The antique folding screen (which Gabriella found in a flea market) is similarly functional, and can divide the space or add privacy as necessary.

an architect's loft in new york

Situated on the top floor of an old industrial building, this light and airy loft belies its location on the corner of one of New York's busiest crossroads. The original ceiling remains in place and is punctuated with large skylights (opposite). The vast windows at the front of the building create a bright setting for the modern-retro furniture which includes two day beds by Charlotte Perriand and Jean Prouvé.

At the intersection of Broadway and Canal Street, Neil Logan and Solveig Fernlund live on one of the most chaotic corners in New York, but it's all too easy to forget that as soon as you enter their light and spacious loft.

Neil and Solveig, both architects, have created a sanctuary of calm on the top floor of an old commercial warehouse building. They share a successful practice, which they run from one half of the space, while the other half is their home, where they live with their young son, Arvid.

As a place to live and work, situated as it is at the crossroads of SoHo, Tribeca, Chinatown and Little Italy, the loft is hard to beat for location. Built in the late 19th century, the warehouse boasts a wall of windows facing Broadway and Neil and Solveig's loft, occupying an entire floor, encompasses the whole frontage.

With more windows at the back of the building and on one side, it is flooded with light anyway, but its position on the top floor, with two large skylights, supplements that further still.

Solveig moved to New York in 1981, having studied art history in Lund, Sweden, and Neil just a year later. He studied architecture at the Rhode Island School of Design and Columbia University, New York. The pair opened their architectural office together in 1993.

'New York was a much more interesting place to live then,' says Neil. 'We were both attracted by the colourful people and culturally progressive environment. The East Village Art scene was in full swing and created a festive mood.'

Having lived on the Lower East Side for almost ten years, by the late 1990s the couple found the neighbourhood gentrifying rapidly and they quickly grew disenchanted. 'It became more commercial and popular, with higher rents, more bars and tourists as a result,' says Neil. They looked for a new place to live and moved to this loft in 1998.

Neil and Solveig needed to make the space functional, while maintaining its intrinsic qualities and keeping structural interventions to a minimum. As is common practice for professionals in New York, Neil and Solveig rent their space. It is convenient and flexible, but it does mean that dramatic architectural changes are out of the question. They have, however, made optimum use of a great starting point.

The loft is reached by an elevator, which opens directly into the floor. There is no lobby area so Neil and Solveig have needed to organize the space so that the most public area, the office, is at the front and is the first thing that visitors encounter on coming out of the lift. The most private spaces, the living areas and the bedrooms, are in the back.

The original ceiling, in a pressed tin style that is now very sought after, needed to be left intact, and as such there are no ceiling-mounted fixtures in the loft. The architects were also keen to make partitions between the spaces that would not block the light too much and avoided putting in doors, explains Neil.

The walls and ceilings are painted white, with grey painted floors. Everywhere the texture of the original surface has been allowed to shine through: the grain of the ply floors, the reliefs on the ceiling.

The architecture studio and the living rooms are furnished simply. Set pieces of classic modern furniture are arranged in groupings, a now conventional way of furnishing such large spaces, but originally a fashion coined by the famous Spring Street loft apartment, just around the corner, where artist Donald Judd once lived.

The architects are well versed in design history and theory, and have picked their furniture carefully. Where they have had the opportunity they have acquired original pieces by designers whose work fits with their own modern aesthetic sensibilities, such as their two daybeds by Charlotte Perriand and Jean Prouvé, two of the most influential designers of the early modern

movement. Elsewhere Neil and Solveig have chosen bookshelves designed by Danish designer Mogens Koch as their standard storage, while industrial felt rugs on the floor create tidy zones of warmth.

Neil and Solveig's distinctive style evolves from their understanding of the necessary functions of the space. The architects have worked to keep a pleasant flow from one area to the next, something that is helped along by the natural light that penetrates every corner. The end result is clean and uncluttered yet unpretentious and personal.

The kitchen area, as just one example, is (to use Solveig's word) 'humble', but very practical to cook in. 'By having open shelves you never have to open cabinet doors when you need something,' says Solveig. 'It's user friendly.'

Opening onto the living room, and with a large dining table at its centre, this is the space in which the family spend much of their time. The skylights above give direct overhead lighting, which marks the 'room' from the rest of the loft, creating a different dynamic and more privacy.

Neil and Solveig keep clutter down with what Solveig describes as 'regular purgings' – which they keep from becoming too epic by standing by a general rule of never letting things accumulate.

'Our mantra is that if you've forgotten you own something then it should probably be thrown away,' says Solveig. In this way they find they can be modest in terms of equipment and gadgets – for example, they have never owned a television or a dishwasher – and still create a warm and comfortable environment.

'It's important to question conventional solutions and arrive at your own formula, there are no given answers, only your personal needs,' Solveig points out. 'It's a long process, but it constantly changes according to our inspiration.'

Neil and Solveig are passionate collectors of vintage classics. The chairs shown here are grouped around a large, industrial, felt rug, which marks out their sitting room. The dramatic 1950s tubular steel chair by Hans J. Wegner (opposite) is a particularly treasured example.

Both architects, Neil and Solveig have divided their apartment to give them two large, open spaces – one for living in and one for working. The strict discipline they exercise to keep out clutter, as well as their marked respect for strong, classic design can be seen throughout both spaces. In the kitchen area (right) open shelves instead of cupboards mean that not only is the beautiful collection of vintage crockery displayed, but it is easily accessible.

The working space (right) includes areas for socializing, too, reducing the temptation to merge home and office life. The bedrooms (below) are kept low and calm, the only decoration being the fabrics, and necessary bedside lamps.

an artist's warehouse loft in marseille

Françoise Martinelli teamed up with friends in the 1980s to buy a space in an enormous old warehouse building. The open-plan living area (right) is large enough to house Françoise's grand piano as well as a large table frequently used for entertaining. One of two tables that were already in the loft when she moved in, Françoise adapted this one to make it into a coffee table by removing the legs and replacing them with giant castors.

Françoise Martinelli, a painter, has lived in her spacious warehouse loft since 1991. She joined forces with a group of friends, including two other painters and a photographer, and together they bought up an entire floor of an ancient, austere building in what was then a run-down quarter of Marseille.

With their limited resources, the five divided the building into live-work apartments for each of them, and formed a creative community with plenty of soul and panache. Compared with today's swanky but too often bland loft environments, the results of their ingenuity and integrity are inimitable but inspiring.

When she moved in Françoise knew she had her work cut out for her. 'There was no toilet and no electricity, I had to fix everything and make everything myself,' she recalls. 'And I had very little resources, so I could only do what was absolutely necessary in order to live.'

The space, which measures an impressive 4,100 sq ft (380 sq m), is split over two levels. Françoise lives in the two rooms that make up the upper floor: a large, open-plan kitchen, a dining and sitting room, dominated by a stunning grand piano, and a bedroom with a bathroom. From the main living space she can access her studio below via a small flight of stairs.

françoise martinelli

Françoise's dynamic abstract paintings, which she will often make in series, are as integral to her apartment as any piece of furniture. The paintings provide a striking focus for the white walls where they are hung or propped up. Her inspiration comes, she says, from 'everything and everywhere'.

Much of her work involves collage, and close study of the works reveals scraps of things she has come across, such as sticks, twigs and photographs. She also includes newspaper articles that have made an impression on her. If she finds, say, an upsetting story about a war – 'There are always wars in the world' – she puts it in her work to help her to exorcise it. 'It helps me to remember, but also to forget.'

This approach is echoed in one of the loft's most fascinating and enchanting features: the floor. The warehouse – or at least the area of it that Françoise now inhabits – used to be a workshop for the construction of leather goods. 'They made everything from handbags to shoes and belts here,' she says. Not having the means to do otherwise, the leatherworkers laid the crude factory floor using whatever they could find to fill the

The warehouse previously housed a leather workshop and the intriguing patchwork floor (above and near right) is a remnant from these days, when workers would use anything that they could find to plug the holes in the industrial stone surface – from pieces of wood to random tiling in assorted shapes, sizes and colours. Françoise has continued the tradition and often makes little reparations herself. The space is so large that Françoise has created a different atmosphere in the living room area by painting a corner red (below, right). The dining area (opposite), next to the kitchen, consists of a large table left in the loft from when it was a workshop.

holes. The result is a beautiful patchwork of large marble slabs, chunks of wood, scraps of metal and several different types of tiles, some ceramic, some terracotta, some hexagonal, some square. 'There were several areas where there were still holes when I moved in,' says Françoise, 'but I thought the end effect of what the workers had done was so beautiful, so I decided I would add to it, rather than start again. I used everything I found, in all sorts of colours.'

Elsewhere the loft's fabric has been left just as Françoise found it – from the windows ('They are so old, the wood is in very bad condition') to the doors (there are none). In keeping with the open simplicity of the space, there is not even a door separating the bedroom from the living space. 'But that's how I like it,' says Françoise.

All the furniture in the loft is *la récupération*. Recycled or found pieces have been given to the owner by her friends, or bought at flea markets. Other items, however, Françoise discovered in the warehouse when she moved in. There are, for example, three chests of drawers – including one very large one, which is put to good use in the kitchen – that were once used by the leatherworkers to store their tools, buckles and threads.

Also inherited was the enormous table in the living area. Françoise made this her own with a single coat of grey paint, and now she dines at it and entertains her friends around it.

Adapting the old to better meet her needs is something the artist excels at. Françoise customized two more tables in the main room by sawing off the legs to make them lower and then adding chunky castors to the feet. Et voilà – two ordinary workshop tables made both flexible and chic.

For seating at these newly low tables, Françoise made cushions from old post bags. She also made use of the versatile heavyweight sacking for curtains elsewhere in the apartment. (If you look closely, it is possible to see scraps of post bag in some of her paintings, too). The little grey chairs – from a flea market – appear to have been salvaged from a church. 'I don't like wood,' she says, 'so I paint everything – in white or grey usually.'

A slender, elegant Frenchwoman, Françoise lives a disciplined life around good homecooking and enjoying the cultural scene of Marseille – frequenting its many theatres and galleries whenever she's not entertaining at home.

An advantage of such a sizeable living space is that it can house Françoise's 1930s grand piano without any risk of overcrowding. A treasured possession since her sixtieth birthday, 'All my friends clubbed together to raise enough money to buy it for me, because I so adore piano music,' she recalls, citing her particular favourites as Schubert, Beethoven and Debussy.

'Although I still don't play myself, I love to have people round who do, and will invite people to listen.' The loft lends itself wonderfully to entertaining, and every summer Françoise's daughter and grandchildren come from Paris to stay. Unsurprisingly, 'They love it here,' she says.

Françoise's bedroom is painted bright white, from the floorboards to the old beams on the ceiling, and contains minimal furniture. All the chairs and tables in the loft have also been painted, albeit in neutral, pale colours, as the artist prefers the look to bare wood. This collage painting (opposite), on the bedroom wall, is one of Françoise's own works.

an apartment in the old port of marseille

This old church clock face (above, left) has no hands and is loved by Hervé because of its suggestion that, within this loft apartment anyway, time has stopped. A typical example of Hervé's animal paintings hangs above his desk (above, right). The kitchen (opposite), as seen from the living room, is both organized and creative – painting tools are stored alongside kitchen equipment. Hervé has stretched thin white sheets of cotton over the units in place of cupboard doors. The mezzanine overlooks the main area of the studio (below), giving the best view of the old 'tomettes' that line the floor.

There is no view from Hervé Maury's compact studio, but you don't need to see outside to know where you are. The particular brightness of the light that permeates the space, the incessant sound of the seagulls and the low hum of passing ferries all feel so specific to the seaside location that it would be impossible to imagine it existing anywhere else.

The loft, where Hervé lives and works as a painter and illustrator, is situated on the second floor of one of the oldest buildings in Marseille. Facing the Old Port, this

area is the hub of the city, lined by quays, filled with fishing boats and yachts, and the centre point of a network of busy streets all teeming with seafood restaurants, terrace cafés and shops. A fish market is held nearby every morning of the week.

The apartment was built during the reign of Louis XIV, who had begun the development of Marseille in 1660 and expanded the docks to provide accommodation for the 20,000 seamen and galley men in the years that followed.

Today, with its luxuriously high ceilings and the extra space created with the addition of a mezzanine, the studio belies its humble beginnings. Unpretentiousness still pervades the space, however, and the availability of a simple, basic life in the centre of the city was exactly what first attracted Hervé.

Hervé was born in Paris and raised in Toulon, a Mediterranean military port, but when he moved into the apartment in the late 1990s it seemed the ideal place – somewhere with enough space to allow him to relax and be imaginative, creative and productive, and yet the city was large and industrious enough to enable him to establish his career without compromise. Living alone, when he's not travelling or exhibiting his work in galleries around France, he spends all his time there.

Hervé has decorated his own front door with one of his leopards (below). Looking back at the bedroom mezzanine and the living room from the main entrance area (right). Hervé sourced most of the furniture in the loft from Marseille's well-stocked flea market. He has mixed pieces in different styles, from different cultures and periods without it appearing messy.

Before he owned the studio it was occupied by a printing business, which specialized in producing labels for popular Provençal soaps and bottles of regional olive oils. To turn it into a home, Hervé had to install water, electricity, heating – for which he bought a wood-burning stove – and insulation. Upstairs, on the mezzanine level, he has made a comfortable bedroom with a small bathroom in one corner. On the lower floor the kitchen, which he built himself, opens out into the living and dining room area.

Repainting was a necessity, he explains, but otherwise decoration has been kept to a minimum. 'It wasn't really an option, I had no money. Instead I collected everything I owned already, things I had found or accumulated over time and on my travels. There's no special theme or agenda otherwise.'

The colours, accordingly, are fairly neutral throughout the studio, made up from a palette of white walls, wood

Behind the stairs (below) a big leather armchair provides a comfortable place to sit and read, next to a wall of bookshelves. Hervé's shelves look tidy and interesting, without being overly ordered or prescribed.

and the sandy tones of his animal paintings. The warm and friendly atmosphere in the space is largely due to the proliferation of these images, which hang on, or lean against, almost every available wall. Portraits of horses, fish, polar bears and so on, his style is unmistakable and the surprised, bright, animated eyes that are his trademark stare out from each one, at once making the rooms feel full of amiable character.

Here and there Hervé's found curiosities, his inspirations, are displayed and serve further to illustrate his own sense of humour: a brace of antlers above the kitchen shelves, a lifebuoy ring hung on the bedroom wall. His

personal favourite, he says, is a large clock which once belonged to an old church in Provence. 'It doesn't have hands anymore, and so won't tell the time, but I like that,' he says. 'Time is stopped here, there's no rush. Leave that outside.'

Art and life are inseparable: Hervé's paint brushes hang neatly over the kitchen sink, below the shelf of wine glasses, which are just as tidily arranged. And his canvases are stacked all around the studio.

Hervé finds that children, particularly his young nieces, seem to like the apartment especially. 'To them I suppose it looks like a playground. That's fine, though, and there's almost nothing fragile or precious in any way.' Except the black leather Le Corbusier chaise longue, perhaps.

As a large port with easy access to Corsica and Tangiers, it's relatively easy to find exotic and interesting 'antiquities' in Marseille. Its flea market is arguably one of the best in France – a country renowned for its flea markets – and the city's most eclectic retail outlet, attracting bargain hunters from far and wide looking for antiques, bric-à-brac, books and clothes; much of Hervé's furniture comes from here.

Children aside, the artist himself finds much to love about his living arrangement. 'When I stop working, I can be in bed in five minutes,' he says. 'It's the same when I'm in bed and I wake up. I go to bar de la marine downstairs, look out at the port and the day begins!'

Hervé also finds himself constantly entertaining friends in the flat. Perfectly placed to explore and experience the city should they want to venture out, it's a great place for people to visit him from Paris for the weekend.

Most of all, though, it's the feeling of security that Hervé likes best about the building, 'Oddly, I don't feel like I am the owner of this place, but instead I feel lucky to be able to spend a little time here,' he explains. 'I feel so secure, so quiet, even though there is no luxury and it all seems so basic. I think the real comfort of the place comes from a more traditional way of living; from the ritual of bringing in wood up two flights of stairs every time I need to stock up for winter, from the holes in the tiles on the floor, from the absence of an oven to cook on, which means I must make my meals on the gas rings.'

The bedroom on the mezzanine level (above) has a small bathroom in one corner (left), where Hervé has used clever positioning of spotlights to create a different atmosphere from the rest of the room. Simple, white, cotton covers – like those in the kitchen – have been used on the cupboards here, too.

a clifftop cabin in mallorca

A sunny terrace next to the kitchen overlooks the sea (above, left). You can take a shower there and enjoy the view and, as there is no railing and it's a steep drop to the rocks below, that can be quite an invigorating experience. A sandy beach lies just out of view to the right (above, right). Looking through the arch towards the end of the kitchen (below, right), where there is a large fireplace on one side and the original well on the other — a detail of which can be seen opposite. The door, just to the right of the well, leads out to the terrace.

Tony Montaner has been living in Mallorca for the best part of two decades. A keen entrepreneur, however, he has never stayed still for long — constantly lured by the promise of travel.

Only partly down to a healthy sense of adventure, Tony's wanderlust has more to do with his humanitarian work. Describing himself as being 'like Robin Hood, but in Mallorca!', recently he has been dividing his time between the island and a small fishing village in Madagascar, where he is very involved in a scheme to supply clean water to the locals, to raise money to help complete the local hospital and to teach craft skills to enable self sufficiency.

Using his creativity and curatorial skills where he can, his work has also extended to the staging of an exhibition of photographs of the local craftswomen, all proceeds were given back to the village.

Tony is an active member of the cosmopolitan artists' circle on Mallorca. He used to have an art gallery in the 1980s and subsequently made a deal, buying an old farm which he transformed into five artist's studios. Entirely rent-free, he describes the studios as being 'comfortable, but not luxurious: it's the typical way

of living on the island — even for the tourists.' His beach house is situated on a cliff, which happens to overlook an exceptionally beautiful stretch of the coast, and would make most people dream of making it their home. Tony renovated an outhouse: a tiny rectangular building — possibly once a garage or tool shed which was occupied only by a pig and some sheep, and a lot of debris.

With a little work and a little vision, the result is a very comfortable and charming beach house. It consists of a kitchen and a bedroom, the two rooms only partly divided by the large archway, while a terrace, right at the cliff edge, makes for amazing views, and there is a direct route down to the sandy beach nearby.

It's not luxurious, but it doesn't need to be. 'I just fitted it out in the most modest way possible,' says Tony. 'In the end, I just want a simple life!'

After cleaning everything ('I had to get rid of the pig, it smelled'), Tony cleverly adapted the space to include bathroom facilities between the two rooms, and a simple kitchen with storage and a gas stove.

Most of the paintings in the house are works that Tony exhibited at the gallery, buying them from the artists after it closed. The minimal furniture is from Java or from the Spanish mainland. Beyond the necessities, however, the building's original details provide plenty of aesthetic value: the ornate grates on every window, for example, which were installed 'probably to protect the women workers indoors,' explains Tony.

The distinctive archways, meanwhile, are typical of the region. Betraying its humbler beginnings as an outhouse, the corrugated iron roof is still in place.

A large fireplace also remains, opposite a very basic well in the kitchen. Though the former is still fully functioning and provides welcome heating in winter months, the well would have once been used for drinking water. 'Even fifty years ago life in this region was very basic, not civilized at all,' says Tony. 'There was no electricity even until quite recently.'

Although the well is no longer necessary, Tony has left this particular piece of history in place. Now with fully functioning plumbing and those seaviews to be taken advantage of, he has also surpassed the need for a bathroom by installing an outdoor shower on the terrace.

Tony – himself a great cook – has built a basic kitchen consisting of just a small stovetop and a number of open shelves. Ornamental shutters on the windows are different in each room, but were there when Tony first found the house and it was occupied by farm animals. The door on the left leads out to the terrace. Through the archway he has installed an indoor shower adjacent to the bedroom. The bedroom itself is reached by a single step and is kept minimal, with plain cotton fabrics and a mosquito net.

The bedroom (opposite and above, left) is furnished with simple country chairs and its window looks out over the sea. In the kitchen (above, right and below, right) Tony has hung a curtain with a striking black graphic. It can be closed over the open terrace doors on a hot day – useful if there is a strong sea breeze. All the art in the house, including this portrait of a Native American, is by artists who exhibited in Tony's gallery.

Lili and Jesko built much of the furniture in the apartment themselves. In the bathroom and kitchen they constructed cupboards from simple wooden frames and decorative punched metal panels (above). Old glass doors and windows (right) separate the rooms in the basement apartment and allow light to travel through. Lili painted the *Burmese Woman Selling Fish* in 2005. Here you can see into the kitchen from the dining room. When Lili and Jesko moved in they took up the lino on the floors and sanded the floorboards. In the kitchen and bathroom they painted an old tile trompe-l'oeil onto the cement.

When Lili Nalõvi and Jesko Willert first moved into their basement flat in Harvestehude, Hamburg, it looked very different from how it does now. 'The wooden floor was hidden under lino-laminate and the cement floor in the bathroom and kitchen was covered over,' recalls Lili. 'The ceilings were covered with polystyrene, the walls were covered with disgusting wallpapers and the old glass panels were all covered with wood.' The stucco reliefs were hidden under a thick coat of paint.

There was not even a shower, 'and in the kitchen there was only a sink and a stove, while the walls were tiled with cardboard.' Luckily, Lili and Jesko, both artists, had vision. They quickly saw the apartment's potential and because of its state they were able to rent it cheaply, despite its large size (1055 sq ft; 98 sq m) and sought after location.

The apartment occupies the basement of a late 19th-century villa. 'It is a typical posh, Hanseatic tradesman's villa,' says Jesko. 'This is one of Hamburg's most exclusive neighbourhoods and it is famous for these beautiful, expensive villas.' Lili and Jesko use the apartment as their workshop, showroom and, although they travel

extensively, as their home, too. 'We paint here, we build our furniture here, it has to be a space where clients, photographers and film productions can come and go.'

The pair found the apartment while they were studying at the art school in Hamburg. 'We noticed the charming atmosphere of the flat straightaway,' says Lili, 'with the old wooden floorboards and the stucco relief on the ceiling and the original glass doors and windows, which separate the rooms and lend a magical light to the space.'

They gradually stripped back the layers and rediscovered the building's original features. An ongoing job, the coats of paint on the stucco reliefs took days of washing to remove and the pair decided to leave them as they were once the paint had come off. Having stripped the old wallpapers, they hung their own handprinted wallpapers, on Japanese ricepaper, and in some places used glazing techniques, decorative plasterworks and – on the ceilings – more trompe-l'oeil.

Lili and Jesko designed their own tables, bed and wardrobe, while other pieces have been adapted to suit their needs. One old Indian glass cupboard, which the pair bought from an antique dealer, was not tall enough. 'We built our own extra cupboard and assembled the two together,' says Jesko. 'Nobody would notice that there is an old and a new part to the cupboard, they work so well together.' Nearly all the lampshades are homemade, too, says Lili. 'Mostly they are handprinted Japanese ricepaper or pleated silk with sequins and pearls.'

The overall impression of the Hamburg apartment can strike awe into the unsuspecting visitor. 'People stand there with their mouths open, like fish in an exotic aquarium!' says Jesko. 'There are so many details to look at and there is so much to discover.' This is equally the case with visitors to their exhibitions who find themselves immersed in a new world.

'You wouldn't expect this mystical light and special atmosphere in a basement,' adds Lili. 'But we wanted to transform the flat into an oasis, and the rooms into paintings.'

The large dining room is lined with Lili's own paintings (from left to right, *Early Morning Cheeroot*, *Chiyo with Rose*, *Burmese Woman Coming from Taungbi Market* and *El Tocador de Margarita*) and features several of their beautiful handmade lampshades. The two hanging above the table are made from handprinted Japanese ricepaper, while the one in the far corner is constructed from pleated silk. Just seen on the far right of the room, the radiator is hidden under a simple wooden frame with punched metal panels in the same style as the cupboards in the kitchen and bathroom.

The artists have another studio in Sicily
and also travel to Asia, South America
and India. They try to take something
home from every journey. Handprinted
wallpaper on Japanese ricepaper covers
the glass door panels and the walls
in Lili's studio (opposite). A work in
progress, Lili and Jesko are creating this
wall hanging (above) by painting
straight onto silver leaf. The oil on
canvas, *Smoking Burmese*, was painted
by Jesko.

In a quiet, rural area the front and back doors of this house open directly onto the countryside. Jane and Olle have amassed a covetable collection of traditionally Swedish antique furniture (opposite) over the years. Rebuilding the house themselves meant that they could adapt the house to fit the furniture, so decoration and furnishing was less of a task than it might have been.

olle olsen and jane myhran

Olle Olsen and Jane Myhran live in a sheep house in Skåne, a choice predominantly determined by their dog. It was, says Jane, by and large, their big, beautiful mongrel Smilla's decision.

Jane and Olle had decided to downsize when they retired from their antique-dealing business in 2002. They had moved to Skåne from Stockholm some years previously, buying and restoring a large farmhouse, and setting up their antique shop in the barn. Although they were very happy there, the couple found they simply had more space than they really needed and began looking at some local apartments.

'Smilla got very depressed about the whole thing,' recalls Jane. 'At one stage we were thinking about moving into a three room apartment in Ystad. Smilla refused to go in! She just lay down on the street and resisted all the way. Then, when we did finally get her inside, she put her head under a bed and did not move until we went out again.'

Jane and Olle hated to see Smilla (who is named after the protagonist in Peter Høeg's popular novel, Miss Smilla's Feeling for Snow) so upset, so they resumed their hunt, this time with some of her priorities in mind, and settled eventually on a little sheep house back in Skåne.

Surrounded by fields and a forest, complete with sheep and rabbits, there is plenty of space for large dogs like Smilla to enjoy around the new property. Happily settled there now, Jane and Olle are fond of telling Smilla's story and say they are ever grateful that she acted the way she did: 'She is the smartest of us three, for sure,' says Jane.

The idea of 'downsizing' is a little misleading, however. Jane and Olle had completed the work on their previous farmhouse and were in fact just keen to get started redeveloping, renovating, building and redecorating somewhere new.

In the large sitting cum dining room, which adjoins the kitchen (opposite), the absence of a sofa means that all meals and socializing take place around this large, antique table (below). Throughout the house, the mix of rustic and Gustavian furniture – such as this paint-decorated folk bench and the two simple antique-white dining chairs – provides an attractive contrast of colour and design against the consistently pale wood floors and limewashed stone walls.

When they bought the house in Skåne there were just two rooms and a kitchen. The stables, which joined up to the house, also shared the house roof. Although they knew it probably wouldn't be large enough for all their needs as it was, it was surrounded by plenty of land, giving ample scope for extension.

The house was in terrible condition, having been left in a state of disrepair and neglect by the previous owners. But Olle and Jane were not put off. On the contrary, with their experience of restoring their previous home, they saw the potential immediately. Over a period of three years, the couple gradually restructured the space, and it now consists of five reasonably sized rooms as well as the kitchen and a bathroom. As they had no use for the stables as they were so they decided to adapt them and turn them into bedrooms and extra living spaces that would accommodate their guests and extended family when necessary, and that they could enjoy the rest of time.

Although the area has become a popular holiday destination in recent years, increasing the traffic on the nearby roads, the house is situated in a relatively quiet part of the countryside. The front and back doors open directly – via the surrounding, well-tended gardens – onto the fields and woodland.

Old Skåne houses, explains Jane, are usually quite long and narrow, with the rooms connected directly and arranged in a line, allowing the light to permeate the length of the building as efficiently as possible. This one is something of an exception, mainly due to the extension work, but large windows and reflective white walls prevent the region's short daylight rations in winter from being a problem.

Experienced enough not to have to rely on an architect, the couple both entirely designed and built the new structure themselves. The whole process took about two years to complete, but Olle and Jane were determined to bring out the beauty and originality in 'this old, sick house'.

The house is, naturally, furnished with pieces that the couple has collected over the three and a half decades that they spent dealing antiques. Every now and then something would come along that they weren't able to sell on, and it is these gems that make up almost every item in the house. Everything has its own story.

All the furniture, and most of the accessories and decorative touches, too, says Jane, are also very typically Swedish. It is this commonality, most likely, as well as

different reasons. It is special to the couple for its functionality, for what it represents: 'We have spent so many happy times around this table with our friends and family,' says Jane. 'It is big enough for twelve people to sit around it, and if you sit down at this table for dinner you will find that you have to stay there for the whole evening. We have no sofa in the house, and it is always a nice way to be with people around the table. And everyone seems to like it.'

The rough stone walls have been limewashed white in every room of the house. New bleached wood floors, meanwhile, keep the feeling throughout light and airy. The background is neutral and natural, and it allows each individual item — whatever type of wood or whatever colour, or however decorative it happens to be — to stand out proudly against it.

Their way of life and their past profession are ultimately what has enabled Olle and Jane to put together such an interesting and eclectic home. Although the business of antique dealing would often suggest otherwise, there is never any risk of clutter. Their secret has been in their ability to keep the house furnished with the bare minimum: things they both love and need.

The furniture comes from different regions and periods, but is all typically Swedish — down to the Dala horses in the window of one of the bedrooms (right) converted from the old stables. And although it is principally made up of antique pieces, the mix still lends the house a contemporary feel. Olle has made use of the attic space of the house by turning it into a bedroom (opposite). The legs of the antique chair are an old tree branch. As is the case in several houses featured in this book, Olle and Jane have used rag rugs — a basic but traditional way to add warmth and comfort to bare floors.

their particularly judicious placement, that makes each piece work coherently.

It is doubtless, however, that Olle and Jane have the knack so common to antique specialists — to make the objects and the furniture in the house all the more beautiful through their canny arrangement and juxtaposition of styles, colours and periods — from rustic, once brightly painted cupboards such as those in the kitchen, to stylish antique-white traditionally Gustavian pieces elsewhere.

The best-loved piece of furniture is a large, sturdy and very heavy pine table dating from around 1700. Not ones to be precious about monetary or even historical value for its own sake, Jane would like their house to give the impression that, 'We are different people, we are not modern at all, and we are not fussy about social status or showing off', the table takes pride of place, therefore, for

The unusual house that Ramon Pujol Roca and David Anadon Escoda share in Menorca is called Es Galliner for a very good reason. Until as recently as 1997 it was a henhouse.

The little henhouse sat on a traditional Menorcan Tanca, an uncultivated plot of land – its resident chickens long since departed. Not far from it was a cistern building, another basic structure, of similar size. And in a flash of inspiration Ramon, who was visiting the area while on a holiday, saw their potential.

At the time Ramon was very successfully working as a window dresser and subsequently as an interior designer in Barcelona. He investigated the henhouse's background and decided to make it a weekend home, a place to get away from everyday life. He enlisted the help of his friend to transform the long-abandoned buildings and they started work immediately.

'The idea at the beginning was just that it would be somewhere we could come to when we needed to escape from the city,' says Ramon. 'We never imagined that it might eventually become our home…'

The pair began by building a roof across the henhouse and cistern building, uniting them as one and in doing so creating a new interior space out of the otherwise empty land between. This middle section was the first part of the project to become habitable and became Ramon's temporary home while he worked on the rest of the house. 'For the first year I slept on a camp bed when I came here,' he recalls. 'Of course there wasn't any electricity to start with either – just an ice box and some candles, and torches to light up my lonely nights…!' It was not luxurious by any stretch of the imagination, but the magic of Menorca, its starry skies and the nightly soundtrack of the surrounding wildlife, was more than enough incentive to rough it a little.

Because Ramon was only able to visit and work on the house when he could escape from his hectic lifestyle back in Barcelona, he wanted to keep the work he needed to do to a minimum. The refurbishment plan was simple and the decoration likewise.

The cistern building gradually became the bathroom and two bedrooms, while the 'henhouse zone' now houses a cosy kitchen and an outdoor dining area.

In time Ramon's bolthole became so comfortable and the days and weeks he spent there so restorative and enjoyable that the designer made the decision to move and live here full time in 2002. 'I became addicted to spending the Menorca summer nights watching the

If it weren't for the name, and Ramon and David's addition of little chicken details everywhere, Es Galliner might be unrecognizable as the old cistern building and henhouse that it once was. The entrance to the house (above) is via a rustic Menorcan wooden gate. The kitchen backs onto a shady terrace (opposite) with views over the well-tended garden – when eating outside food and drink can just be passed through the window.

ramon pujol roca and david anadon escoda

stars and listening to the sounds of nature – and all these things are of course just the same as when I first started to come here. It's my home now, more than anywhere else.'

Ramon had to adapt his professional life to the little island. He gave up his job in Barcelona and opened a design boutique and gift shop, La Maravilla, in the centre of Maó.

Es Galliner is filled with accessories from his shop and items that he finds in 'gangaria', a street market, where people sell the things that they don't want any more, held on Sundays in the old airport.

A shady terrace now leads out from the kitchen, where Ramon and David can sit and enjoy the garden, or entertain friends. Filled with typical Menorcan flora and fauna, including a hardy Cyprus tree, the outside environment was at least as much a priority – if not more so – as the house itself when Ramon first started work.

'It took two years to turn the land into a garden, but it was very important – it's one of the things that has made

Ramon needed to install electricity and plumbing into the house and he also put a new cement floor down throughout, shown here in the kitchen where he painted it red (opposite, above). Offsetting the otherwise very minimal interior, Ramon has added unconventional touches such as these two tiles integrated into the wall behind the sink (opposite, below, left), and his many kitsch accessories – often brought home from his shop La Maravilla. The apron (opposite, below, right) is printed with the shop's trademark image – a photograph Ramon took of a donkey.

The small, high, square windows (above, left) are another hint about the house's history, but there aren't many such clues, unless you count the feather lampshade in the dining room (below, right).

the biggest difference here – that makes it like a "real" house.' When friends visit, as they often do, they are frequently inspired by Es Galliner and start making enquiries about similar plots of land that they could think about transforming in the same way.

It was a savvy move at a time when the property market was so difficult to get a foothold in, but, says Ramon, he was lucky to find it when he did. While there are still many plots available to buy like this one, the prices on the island have gone up considerably in recent years.

Ramon and David share Es Galliner with Taca, Ramon's cat from Barcelona, and Dor, a dog that the couple have taken in since they moved. Meanwhile, little chicken references can be spotted everywhere, from the wrought-iron sculpture outside to a feathered lampshade in the dining room.

Ramon and David are proud of the house's history, but at the same time they are happy that it is no longer immediately apparent. 'It's hard to make out the original structure now,' says Ramon. 'You can't tell it was a henhouse and it looks like it was always meant to be like this from the beginning.'

modern flexible living in finland

By the entrance to the apartment (above, left) Ritva has chosen a small table designed by Ulla Koskinen. Above it hangs a textile piece with a pleated effect by Ritva herself. All the glassware on the table (above, right) was also designed by her, for Hadeland. Ritva loves flowers, both when fresh and when used as a decorative element such as in this painting, by Veikko Vionoja (opposite), and on the antique embroidered Russian throw on the wrought-iron sofa that she has made comfy with lots of soft cushions. The ceramic art piece on the floor is by Ritva Tulonen.

Ritva Puotila is a renowned designer and artist, and is creative director of Woodnotes, as well as their principal designer. Woodnotes, a design company, produces textiles – in particular rugs, but also bags, accessories, artworks and other products from paper yarn – that can be found throughout Finland, and increasingly around the rest of the world, too.

Having won many awards for her work and exhibited widely over the years (including appearances in twenty cities in the USA, as well as in Japan, Denmark, Sweden, Norway, Iceland and Finland), Ritva is known in her own right. Her artistic works feature in the collections of many European museums of applied arts and in the collections of the American Craft Museum and in the Design and Architecture Collection of the Museum of Modern Art in New York. Her distinctive one-off pieces of textile art adorn both the headquarters of the Bank of Finland in Helsinki and the Council of the European Union building in Brussels.

As the first to experiment extensively with paper yarn, Ritva is largely credited with starting a fashion for the material. Environmentally friendly and durable, it has a very clean, pure, matt aesthetic and, while usually in neutral colours, it works especially well in traditional, minimalist Scandinavian settings.

Ritva's apartment just outside Helsinki is filled with Woodnotes textiles, as well as other pieces of her work.

Over the years the designer has practised many different types of design and art, in various materials, from wood and glass to ceramic, having dreamt of being an artist ever since she was a small child. Her glassware and ceramics are filled with flowers and displayed on side tables, her rugs lie on the new wooden floors and hang on the sharp, white walls, alongside her artworks and beautiful, original textile hangings.

Ritva and her husband moved into the apartment in the late 1980s, and have always lived in the area. The block itself was built in 1981 and is an important example of modern constructivist architecture and, although it is surrounded by pine forests and near to the sea – 'a typical Finnish view' – it is by no means remote. Ritva's studio and guest room is just next door (allowing her to be flexible about the hours she works), while many of her friends and family also live nearby.

Ritva shares the apartment with her husband and it's quite a different space from the one they moved into all those years ago. They have three sons who live nearby (the youngest is now managing the Woodnotes company) and when they left home they decided to rearrange the interior dramatically. Needing fewer rooms, but more space, they have removed several walls and transformed the apartment into an open, light-filled space.

Arranged around the bathroom, the living area and the library, the sleeping areas all flow into one another, and are separated from the dining room and the kitchen by just a half-width, white wall. Windows run along the entire length of two sides of the apartment. 'Good light is very important for my work,' says Ritva. 'But also for my mind. With these windows you get a real sense of the natural world outside which helps – even when it's cloudy, for example, I can still see the clouds moving. I can see heaven better.'

With a pristine, almost gallery-like interior, decorating the apartment is like covering a blank canvas. And, says Ritva, she changes it constantly. 'A lot of the furniture is black, white and brown, so that makes it easier to change the décor according to how we are feeling,' she explains. 'In the winter I often decorate with red and dark brown art and antiques, but then I'll have new colours in the summer – it's important to me to try different things.'

As well as with her own designs, the apartment is filled with many pieces from different origins. Old and new are mixed together, but everything has been carefully chosen.

Flowers, says Ritva, are the most important thing in her home. 'I have always had to have flowers in my life ever

In the living area (above) Ritva displays carefully chosen works of art such as the painting by Kristian Krokfors, which hangs above her favourite Antonio Citterio-designed side table; a collection of woven baskets on the low storage units which double as seats (right); and a few of her own designs. On the far wall (opposite) hangs a textile piece Ritva wove from paper yarn and straw. The carpet on the floor is her also own design and is a unique piece.

since I was a small child. They give me inspiration, the colours are so indicative of the seasons.' She also uses them a great deal in her own work – one piece she cites as an example is 'Black Roses', which comprises hundreds of dried roses woven into a huge stainless steel mesh.

The designer is an avid collector of glass, which she used to work with herself in the 1980s, and also antique furniture. 'I go to markets to find things that are really special. I also know other collectors who will tell me if something I will like is about to come onto the market, and I go to auctions.'

Proportion is a crucial factor when Ritva is choosing items of furniture. 'The architecture of the apartment defines what you can physically bring in here,' she explains. One of the largest pieces she owns is her black Chinese cabinet – something she found through an antique dealer friend, but otherwise storage consists of several low cabinets that line the walls. 'They are the perfect height, as they don't destroy the line of the windows,' says Ritva. 'You can also use them as extra seating, or you can easily change what you put on the surface if you want to use them as a table.'

Her favourite item of furniture is a contemporary side table by Italian designer Antonio Citterio: 'I like this so much because it is so very simple and flexible. You can move it anywhere and it looks right – it creates such a relaxed feeling.'

Ritva thought hard about the best way to divide the space when she removed the internal walls in favour of a more open-plan and flexible way of living. The low wall was an important intervention. 'I believe the dining table must be separated from the other areas of the apartment, as you must be able to completely relax when you are eating,' she says.

Ultimately, no matter how much Ritva reorganizes the space and changes the decoration, one thing is always paramount in her mind: that it should feel like home. 'Home is where you relax, where you meet your friends, and where you can be totally yourself. Home must be the most wonderful space in the whole world.'

The bedroom (opposite) is very simply decorated, with a contemporary, striped Woodnotes carpet on the floor, contrasting effectively with the almost two hundred-year-old Finnish archipelago rug on the wall. An ethnic textile from Guatemala on the opposite wall in the bedroom (below, left). All the cushions in the bedroom (below, right) and on the terrace are also from Woodnotes, as is the terrace carpet.

a swedish summerhouse by the sea

Situated on a small cliff-top road which leads straight down to the sea, the views from Lena's summerhouse are completely free from obstacles. On a fine day you feel like you might almost be able to see as far as Denmark. The terrace opens out from a bedroom on the second floor (above). The furniture in the living room (opposite) is upholstered in stripes. Lena, a self-confessed 'stripe addict', designs and collects textiles (right).

Lena Rahoult and her husband have spent many summers on the west coast of Sweden and live in Stockholm the rest of the time. Their house, in the small village of Torekov, is on the coast and has been in the family since the 1930s when Torekov was little more than a modest fishing community. These days the charms of the village are more widely known and the area sees a healthy influx of visitors at weekends, but the change is less an issue of tourism and instead has simply served to make the area more lively.

Lena's wooden summerhouse is a former little resort hotel and was probably, she says, constructed in the 1920s to cater for the first generation of holiday makers. Similar in design to many of the other houses nearby, which were mostly built to house the local fishermen, it is situated right on the sea and has wonderful views towards Denmark, while it also benefits from that particular reflected light that is distinct to seaside areas.

'The view and the special light are definitely two of the most instantly appealing aspects of living here,' says Lena. 'You overlook the sea wherever you are in the house. Being so close to the water also means that every morning, no matter what the weather is like, you can always go for a quick swim before breakfast.'

A well-renowned textiles designer, Lena has exhibited several times, both in Sweden and abroad. Her trademark fabrics with bold stripes are represented in the National Museum of Sweden in Stockholm, the Röhsska Museum of Design and Applied Art in Gothenburg and the Musée d'art moderne in Paris.

Lena's husband is a professional bird watcher and their house here provides the perfect base for his occupation – whether observing the seabirds, or writing books about the subject in the calm environment. Certainly, both Lena and her husband take their creative inspiration from the nature that surrounds them. Even Lena's trademark

stripes – although both traditional and geometric – have a rhythm, harmony and natural colour palette that one imagines has much to do with the seaside influences.

Lena has endeavoured to keep the design of the house as straightforward as possible, to facilitate the easygoing life she and her family like to live during the summer months. Their routine fits in with the rest of the village – the pace of affairs in Torekov is relaxed. The emphasis here is on the quality of life, good food, good health and the environment. In Torekov people generally avoid driving in favour of getting around on bicycles, while fresh seafood is always abundant.

The Rahoults' house has two floors and consists of a study, a living room, a dining room, three bedrooms and a kitchen. 'It used to have very small rooms,' explains Lena, 'but when we restored it we realized we didn't need so many. We removed some of the walls and reorganized it so that now we have fewer rooms, but they are bigger.'

The dining room looks out over the sea, and a large second balcony upstairs can be accessed via one of the bedrooms. Spacious and light, Lena painted all the interior walls white and kept pale wooden floorboards throughout.

The fact that the house had been in the family for so long presented its own difficulties. Lena and her husband needed to adapt the space to suit their own lifestyle, but in doing so they also needed to take care not to eradicate the decades of history and memories that made the house a home. 'Our challenge was to keep the atmosphere of this old family house,' says Lena. 'We wanted, and needed, to make it more modern without destroying the original plan.'

All the furniture, inherited from Lena's husband's family, remained in the house. Lena's personal favourite is a large sofa on the veranda in very light birch wood, and originally bought by Lena's grandmother-in-law. Reluctant to part with or change any such memory-filled fixtures, Lena's input into the interior decoration

The view from the living room through the dining room into the office (above), where Lena's husband writes up his research into birds (his book, *Europese Vogels*, can be seen on the table in the living room, see page 141). A collection of shells is arranged on a table (right) – Lena gets much of her inspiration for her fabric designs from nature.

was mostly limited to changing the fabrics. 'There were a lot of wallpapers that we did not like, too, so we painted all the walls white,' she explains.

As a sideline to her design practice, Lena has been collecting striped textiles from different parts of Sweden, particularly from the provinces of Skåne and Dalarna, for many years. The fabrics have been a major source of inspiration in her own design work.

Usually hand-woven linen, some of her samples date as far back as the 19th century, and can be found carefully folded and stacked in cupboards. Stripes, of various dimensions and colours, have provided the main theme of the decoration throughout the house: Lena re-upholstered the majority of the old furniture in her textiles and made cushions and bedlinen from them too. 'I am definitely a stripe addict when it comes to pattern,' she says. 'There are none of my own designs in the summerhouse, but I constantly change the scenery by using my collection of old linen fabrics. They are so beautiful because the colours are soft – the sun has faded them and the texture is a little bit worn out. The colours fit so well with all the blue and grey tones of the nature that surrounds the house.'

Somehow the result of the stripes is never overly nautical or contrived, even in such a seaside location it just looks elegant, harmonious and appropriate. 'There are no heavy fabrics,' she explains. 'In general my attitude to decoration is really to keep things very simple. I like to create a warm, but calm and light atmosphere, to mix different furniture styles.' There is no doubt that she has succeeded here and 'from the grandmother, who is 92, to the granddaughter, who is just 6 months old', her family all love to stay here.

'And no matter what time it is, or what it's like outside, the house always feels warm and light,' says Lena. 'It can be grey, stormy and dark but when you are here it's not important. And it is lovely just to sit in the living room and look out across the sea and to listen to the sound of the waves.'

Two of the three bedrooms in the house (above). The bedlinen is, of course, made by Lena, who breaks up the uniformity of the stripes everywhere by mixing the colours and the widths.

The kitchen (above) was one of the rooms in the apartment that Susanne needed to renovate when she moved in, but she did the minimum, replacing the existing units with a simply painted, classic white and wood design. An unusual floorplan dispenses with corridors in favour of connecting rooms (opposite). The living room, here, looks through into the dining room and beyond that, a bedroom. The apartment's original features – such as the Kakkel stove in the corner of the living room – are still in place. Keeping the same colour scheme throughout, with bright white walls and floorboards painted in a soft grey, gives the apartment a sense of coherence and unity.

susanne rützou

Entering Susanne Rützou's light-flooded apartment always has the same effect on her guests. 'Everyone is overwhelmed when they walk through the door,' she says. 'They walk in and go "aaahh", because it's so light and bright, and you don't expect that when you're coming up the stairs.'

Susanne, a successful fashion designer, shares the lakeside apartment in Copenhagen with her husband and their two children. The family moved here from their very central apartment next to Susanne's studio and shop in the fashion district. They felt the need for 'a bit more space and a bit more peace'. Hardly rural, it is still buzzy and convenient – only a not-so-strenuous ten-minute bike ride to work – but more residential and an easier place to live.

Apart from the light, the most immediately striking aspect of the space is its size. At 340 sq m (3600 sq ft), with eight rooms, it is unusually large for a central apartment, 'All the rooms are big, some are huge,' says Susanne. The layout, too, is unusual for a Danish apartment. Rather than arranging the rooms in a line along a long corridor, starting at the entrance with a big room and finishing at the other end with the kitchen as is most common, here all the rooms are connected to each other. There is not really a corridor to speak of, and the five main rooms – all interconnected – face the lake. The other side overlooks an old cemetery.

Even though there is no garden, the apartment has far-reaching views over the tree tops. Nature, as well as light, is important to Susanne, not only in her practical design work (successful and busy, she often works at home too), but also for inspiration. 'My work belongs in Scandinavia,' she explains. 'There is such a particular climate – life here is very dependent on the light, with very long days in summer and a lot of darkness in winter, and my work is quite frequently influenced by the weather.'

Besides replacing the bathroom and adapting the kitchen, the couple didn't have much work to do to the apartment. 'We just painted it,' says Susanne. 'Just' being an understatement when you're talking about a 340 sq m apartment. To maximize the light, all the rooms are white and the floorboards are a pale, warm shade of grey.

The hardest part of implementing any decorative theme beyond this, however, has been reaching an agreement with the rest of the family. Susanne's husband, an architect, favours a strictly minimalist aesthetic, while 'I like older things,' she explains. 'I like to surround myself with things that have a soul, and I like to collect things too. So it's been quite difficult like that – we've had to find a balance.'

They've had to find a balance with the furniture, too. 'It's not supposed to be an exhibition, we have children. It's important that everything is functional and good quality. We do have a few things from IKEA – useful, neutral things,' she admits. 'It's very costly to furnish so many square metres!'

An old cupboard is one particular source of contention. 'My husband hates it, but to me it's an old friend and I can't get rid of it. It was a very impulsive thing that I did a long time ago, late at night when I was about twenty – I was trying to take the paint off it, but the inner layer was oil paint and I was getting very frustrated with it. I just ended up writing this French poem all over it. I always intended to paint over it the next day, but then I found I rather liked it. It tells a story and it reminds me of a lot of things, of other places that I've lived, and times in my life.'

Against the neutral background Susanne can indulge her fashion sensibilities and change details and colours each season by adding new cushions, pictures and accessories. 'It's very easy to change quickly,' she says. As well as keeping the colour scheme constant throughout the apartment, the couple also replaced all the handles on all the old doors with the same Arne Jacobsen design. With twenty-nine doors to attend to, it was a detail that made a big difference.

An old mirror in the bedroom (above)
and an array of African masks (opposite)
reveal Susanne's passion for collecting.

The architect and fashion designer share a love of Japanese paper lampshades, seen here (right) hanging in one of the children's bedrooms. 'It is one thing we agree on,' she laughs, 'but we get through a lot of them – they are not so practical with small children!'

There are three bedrooms and a guestroom in the spacious apartment. Despite both being successful designers (one of Susanne's dresses hangs on a mannequin here, left), the couple have not wanted to reorganize the apartment structurally.

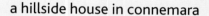
a hillside house in connemara

Surrounded by beautiful hills, the house has been painted to blend harmoniously with the landscape (above, left). Looking through from the bathroom into one of the house's original bedrooms (above, right). Natural wood features everywhere, as in this bedroom (opposite), and it is rare to see anything painted (let alone plastic or synthetic) here.

The first time Mari Saville explored what is now her house in Connemara, there were cattle grazing in the kitchen. The building had sadly fallen into disrepair after the first owner had died in 1928. The house had a fascinating history, having been designed and built in the late 19th century by the brother of the former British Prime Minister Ramsay McDonald, who was a doctor in the area.

Mari was born in Cork and schooled in Dublin. She enrolled at Columbia University in New York, before quickly deciding against the idea and falling into the theatre instead. She returned to Britain five years later to study sculpture in London at the Chelsea School of Art. It was during her time there that she decided she really wanted to get back to her roots. 'I went to Connemara for a weekend. It's a place where my parents had a long connection – they would go there for fishing and so on – and I decided it was where I wanted to live,' she explains. 'While I was searching for a cottage, I kept seeing this old ruin on a hill overlooking a bay. It was a big, square thing. It had no roof, no windows, and a huge "ban the bomb" sign scrawled all over the front.'

A Victorian copy of a Georgian design, with a flat roof set under a pediment, the house could not be less typical of the idyllic Irish ramshackle country pile usually depicted in property magazines, but since Mari took over and began her rescue mission, it has attracted a fair amount of attention. The restoration process has, however, not been without its challenges. 'One of the biggest design problems was the windows and the balcony railing,' she says. 'I drew up the façade and after much fiddling around decided on divisions of eight on the front windows and four on the side and back.' With help from some of her student friends at Chelsea, Mari chose Chinese Chippendale for the railing.

The roof, too, was 'a major piece of work to reinstate,' recalls Mari. 'But I got married at that time and my brother gave me a pre-cast French concrete system as a wedding present, making the whole restoration possible!'

Delighted with the result, she then painted the house in 'a nice easy green' that would help it to blend in with its surroundings.

mari saville

As large as the building appeared to be, there weren't many rooms and most of them were big and very high-ceilinged, making them rather inhospitable during the winter months. Mari decided to add a new wing to the building, giving herself a study, where she spends much of her time, and an extra bedroom and bathroom. 'Now you could get lost in the house,' she says.

Mari used reclaimed materials in the extension to give it the same feel as the rest of the house. It is an approach that she also applies to the furniture – from a bed constructed from beautiful oak branches to the old milk urn that usefully provides a plinth to display a sculpture. 'Almost everything in the house is there for a reason, and says something that I feel is important,' says Mari. 'Nothing is there without consideration and it's all developed along with my life there. I pay a great deal of attention to detail and am making constant creative decisions – but never too seriously!' Much of the furniture came from Mari's own company, Fens Restoration in London.

On one visit a friend remarked that there wasn't a primary colour in the place – something that, although she'd not noticed it herself before, Mari now sees as a source of pride. 'And there's no plastic either!' she laughs.

The large dining room on the ground floor (opposite) is flooded with light, having the luxury of windows on two sides overlooking the garden (right). The amazing stone walls have been left as Mari found them. Through the dining room is the entrance (above) which leads into the living room. Casual, but elegant displays such as a tray of stones on an old table or a piece of driftwood positioned, as if on a plinth, on an old barrel are testimony to Mari's ability to see the beauty in very simple rustic items.

The spacious bathroom (opposite) is very much in keeping with the rest of the house, with stripped wood and antique details such as the stunning cabinet top and mirror. An unusual bed frame (below) has been constructed somewhat crudely from logs, and emphasizes the already strong feeling of being very close to nature in this remote part of Ireland.

a parisian apartment with a view

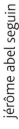
Jérôme worked with an architect to redesign the space in his Parisian apartment, and in doing so has made it unrecognizable from when he first moved in. A slim wooden shelf system (above, left) provides a contained storage solution and desk space along one wall. The kitchen (above, right) fuses with a dining room to the right and a living room in front. The plain white units give a gallery-style setting for the carved wooden figures (right); a souvenir from Indonesia where Jérôme has another house and a workshop. Behind the living room, sliding doors (opposite) open onto a balcony with a near panoramic view of Paris.

Jérôme Abel Seguin's monumental sculptures and furniture, carved from giant pieces of Indonesian hardwood, are internationally renowned. A self-appointed 'pioneer in enhancing raw beauty', Jérôme is an artist and craftsman obsessed with nature and minimalism. Both inform his own surroundings and lifestyle as much as they inspire his work.

Jérôme divides his time between his workshop and home in Indonesia and his minimal apartment in Paris, where he was educated in the beaux arts and at the Ecole Boulle.

He moved here – to a space on the sixth floor of one of Paris's rare, old industrial warehouses – from a ground-floor loft-style apartment in the Bastille, and was instantly enthralled by the extraordinary light and the dramatic views over the city. From the vantage point of the apartment's 50-ft (15 m) long terrace, Jérôme says looking out over Paris is, 'Like being on a vessel bridge sailing above the crest of the city. The view here, by day or night, always provokes an exciting feeling in visitors, too. Suddenly people become quite childlike – recognizing the monuments and remembering where they are in the city.'

Jérôme worked with an architect in order to transform the apartment into the large, open space it is now. The main challenge was how to retain a sense of privacy by

incorporating several smaller rooms off the main living area. 'I also spent a long time reflecting personally on the project before the works started,' he recalls, 'always keeping in mind the words of Malaparte: "I need a house which reflects me".'

One of the apartment's most successful features is the way in which all the comforts of modern living – the appliances and so on – are hidden, leaving an apparently empty space. Like the tables and chairs Jérôme fashions

from single, great slabs of wood, the designer perceives the apartment as one seamless entity: 'I have no favourite room, this flat is for me one space,' he explains.

Jérôme strives for a sense of serenity and stability in his environments. Each of the items of furniture in the apartment is chosen for its design and size rather than names and labels (he says he would rather not know if someone famous designed his chairs or not), Jérôme is concerned with its purity of form and its material.

Given the importance he places on ridding the space of 'clutter', 'fragments' and 'tension', it is surprising that the clean, sharp white lines of his pristine Parisian apartment do not appear harsh or soulless. 'What does it matter if the work is beautiful in configuration, generous in space, free from clutter, sophisticated in details, pure in materials, unless it reveals the soul?'

Far from harsh or soulless – often the criticisms of minimal and white spaces such as this – the artist's own handcrafted furniture, such as a low table in the main living area and the primitive art that he has collected from Indonesia and Africa, lend the flat warmth and character. This is almost certainly because Jérôme chooses each object with the same mantra he repeats while he is creating his sculptures. 'It must provoke not only an emotion, but also a feeling of fulfilment and true sensuality, which makes you immediately feel you want to touch it.'

Jérôme expresses his love for touch and texture readily and often, explaining that, 'In a dehumanised world, I strive for the real and the human.'

In his sculptures he works with the 'flesh' of wood, ever striving to reveal its essence. 'They take a special form and become an object close to the senses – the finished object involves the whole body and the senses.'

In his apartment, just as in the rest of his work, says Jérôme, 'I want my work to make people dream. My work with its massive aspects and apparent simplicity evokes liturgical objects: a bridge between high art, spiritualism and design. There is no further need to compel, the direction becomes clear. It must be a source of pleasure and sensuality, a place to which anybody can come and for a while be free from thinking about what he is going to do.'

During his travels to Indonesia and Africa Jérôme picks up pieces of primitive art, such as this stool (below, left) and the traditional Indonesian fabrics in the bedroom (below, right) that he finds inspiring in his own work. The main items of furniture, meanwhile, are all chosen for their simplicity of form, whether they are vintage pieces or more contemporary finds (opposite).

Although the two chairs in the foreground (opposite) are design classics, and highly collectable, Jérôme takes no interest in designer names, maintaining that he chose them for their beauty and form. One of the designer's own pieces, this low table (below) is typical of his work and celebrates the natural beauty of the wood. Jérôme sells his work internationally and regularly exhibits in New York and Paris.

a modern dutch country villa

Typical of Michael and Marlou's unconventional style, rather than hang an old Dutch oil painting in a heavy gold frame, they prefer to let the bare edges of the canvas provide the mount (above). In the kitchen (opposite), old wooden doors have been used for the cupboards, contrasting unusually with the new wooden walls. This was one of the first times the Smits and Piet Hein Eek, their architect friend, were to use this look, and they went on to repeat it in Michael's Sissy Boy's concept stores all around Holland. The wooden panelling is now one of Hein Eek's trademarks in his commercial designs.

Michael and Marlou Smit live in a villa in the north of Holland, a little way outside Amsterdam. Shared with their three children, Seph, Levi and Maes, four dogs, one cat and some chickens, the family find that, one way or another, it fits all their needs. The couple had grown up in the region and wanted to settle there, and when the villa came on the market in 1994 Michael and Marlou were attracted to it straightaway. Its unusual situation – next to the sea, with sand dunes on one side and woodland on the other – had a lot to do with its appeal.

A modern country house with a pitched roof in the centre, the villa is spread over one floor. However, says Michael, 'It is more beach house than a bungalow. And everyone who comes here thinks it isn't Dutch. It's not traditional in many ways.'

Once they had moved in, Michael and Marlou decided to redesign the villa with the help of a friend from architecture school, Piet Hein Eek, a well-renowned architect. The west side of the house is now 'one big room for living in', with a sitting room, a dining room, an office and a playroom. Every corner is penetrated by sunlight, thanks to Hein Eek's high, glass ceiling.

The east wing is for sleeping, with a very large bathroom, four bedrooms and a dressing room. Every room has access to the garden and the family use the terrace more than any other part of the house.

The villa is filled with their own, very personal mix of flea market finds, antiques, art and furniture they have designed and made themselves. Michael has a jeans brand, Sissy Boy, and Marlou, too, used to work as a very successful stylist; together they have given the house a distinctive, personal look. Worn wood is carefully reappropriated: old doors, recovered from a French château, for example, have been recycled as the doors for the kitchen units; while the huge dining table and panelling on the walls have been carefully, cleanly constructed from layered, collaged scrapwood, and is one of Hein Eek's designs.

Michael and Marlou have been careful to offset the stark modernity of the glass structure with the aged and distressed furniture and fittings. 'The sunken in and bruised texture of old paints gives a lot of our things a loved and lived in look,' explains Michael, who has also applied the principle to the walls, layering paint in different colours to give a similar effect.

Michael describes the house as 'a warm haven of peace.' With easy access to the office, the shops and the beach, it's not surprising that the family are just as happy there as ever. 'It's a gorgeous place,' as he says. 'And it may seem boring, but we live on the sofa. It's so old and lived in and it's not any special designer make or name – we got it eleven years ago, but it fits like a glove around our family.'

In the kitchen (top) a practical blackboard is hung alongside a painting. An artist friend created portraits of the Smits' family dogs in papier mâché (left). Piet Hein Eek's famous scrapwood table in the glass-roofed dining–living area (opposite), surrounded by antique chairs. The sitting room can just be seen behind the large, open shelves.

The main bedroom (below, left and opposite) is next to a huge bathroom (left and below, right). The latter, in polished concrete, has been painted with a very thin layer of paint to create a 'bruised' effect. The bedroom benefits from the newly installed floor to ceiling windows on two sides, making it feel more like a conservatory than a bedroom in the daytime. The light levels can be adjusted with the simple wooden Venetian blinds.

Light is very important to Micheal and Marlou, who have done everything they can to make sure it fills every corner of the house. The children's bedrooms are painted white from floor to ceiling, leaving the bright textiles and toys to add colour. The passion for all things old and worn extends to every member of the family, demonstrated here by the antique school desk in one bedroom, and a beautiful Chinese bed in another.

a family townhouse in amsterdam

Damaged by a serious fire, this Amsterdam townhouse needed serious restoration to transform it into a comfortable family home. The ground floor (opposite) comprises an open kitchen and dining area, which looks out onto a sheltered garden. While the furnishings have been kept as simple as possible to maximize the limited space in this typically tall and narrow house, there is always room for personal touches.

Born and brought up in Finland, Piri Tamminen moved to Amsterdam when she was twenty. She had met her future husband, Cees, during a holiday in the city and decided to stay.

A few years later, in 1972, Piri and Cees bought a five-storey, canal-side mansion. Although they had already been living in the neighbourhood for a number of years, it was a dramatic and ambitious move, leaving their 'quite romantic but not so spacious' 130 sq ft (12 sq m) rented room in a student house.

The famous crescent shape of Amsterdam city centre, and its beautiful ring of waterways, was designed and built over the course of the 17th century. The narrow streets and canals fan out from the centre and are punctuated by picturesque bridges, and lined with characterful tall, skinny houses, with ornate façades crowned with gable tops – of which this is a perfect example.

Most of these city centre houses are exceptionally attractive, but it was perhaps the beautiful and peaceful situation of this one that made Piri and Cees set their hearts on it.

The house was in very bad shape – a fire had almost destroyed the interior on every level. Furthermore, when Piri and Cees found it the house had been abandoned and subject to much neglect, compounding the damage. It was only because of its poor state of repair, however, that the couple were able to afford it. At a time when the onset of children meant most of their friends were moving to more reasonably priced, larger properties in the countryside, Piri and Cees saw the potential of making this house their home for many years to come.

Testimony to the wiseness of their decision, they are still living there thirty years later. Piri works in the field of tourism as a guide and interpreter, having been the director of the Finnish Tourist Board in The Netherlands for many years. Cees has taken early retirement from his teaching position at the university in order to study philosophy. They have three children, all now grown up, and the house has seen a fair slice of life played out within its walls over the last three decades.

Stacked over five different levels, the floors are connected by very steep stairways. High ceilings and large windows at both the front and the back of the

house ensure that though the building is narrow, it is flooded with light. Because of this the rooms seem much larger than they actually are.

The ground floor (and the lowest level), says Piri, is her favourite place in the house. The kitchen, on this floor, faces the street and the canal, while the connecting dining area backs onto a sheltered, cosy garden. 'It's a fine place to meet family and friends, to relax and talk,' she explains. The garden is furnished with a simple table and a few chairs, and the family often sit outside and have meals there in the summer months.

Piri and Cees needed to embark on an ambitious restoration programme when they moved into the building. Making the house liveable in took the couple more than a year to accomplish and involved significant building work. The high ceilings and the narrow layout only added to the challenge.

Beyond the cost and effort of the internal rebuild, Piri and Cees have kept the house as simple as possible. Natural materials and soft colours are used stylishly throughout, although style is never given priority over comfort and ease of use. 'Though we have the perennial problem of storing our books and things,' says Piri, 'that's another one of the reasons we try to keep it simple.' The drive towards minimalism in the furnishings, however, has not been at the expense of personal expression. Piri's collection of old teapots, for example, is displayed tidily on the window sill in the dining room, while flowers, books and pictures throughout show that this house is a lived-in one.

Visitors who come for the first time are almost always struck by the impressive way the interior contrasts with, and yet somehow complements, the house's grand canal façade says Piri. 'There is an intimate quality and atmosphere in and around the house which people don't expect from the outside.'

The first floor living area and home office (opposite), like the kitchen and dining room below, is open and airy. Large windows at the front and back of the house mean that the space is beautifully light, an important factor in making it feel more spacious than it actually is. The bedrooms (below) fill the floors at the top of the house. Steep stairs connect one floor to the next.

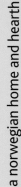
a norwegian home and hearth

As was always the tradition in Norway, the front of the house is painted white, while the back, which looks on to a large backyard, is red and yellow. The reason for this is that white paint was very expensive and many householders used to reserve it for the parts you could see from the street. Stein and IngerLise wanted to be as faithful as they could to the history of the house. Antique benches and boxes (opposite) are presented just as found, with their patina of aged and worn paintwork left, rather than stripped or painted over.

As their friends have been known to comment, Stein Thunberg and IngerLise Hansen's cosy home in Kristiansand resembles 'a tidy flea market'. Given that Stein runs an antique shop, selling objects and furniture he sources himself during their extensive travels around the world, it is perhaps not especially surprising.

Kristiansand is the largest city, and the southernmost one, on the south coast of Norway. There are many 17th-century buildings from its founding days and Stein and IngerLise's charming, old timber house is in the traditional style, typical of the area, in one of a number of blocks in the city centre. They moved to Kristiansand in 1976, when Stein was recruited to play football for the local team, and initially lived outside the city, moving to this house in the mid-1990s.

It was the location that persuaded them to move. 'We love this part of the city,' says IngerLise. 'The house was not very exciting. It was, in fact, very ugly when we bought it. A very old lady had been living here for years and hadn't done anything with it at all, that was easy to see. But it was also not difficult to imagine that it could be great with a little work.'

The work to be done was extensive when they first moved in. All the exterior doors and windows needed replacing, while inside the pair stripped away all the coverings from the walls, floors and ceilings.

The old wooden floors were preserved underneath – 'as they were when they were laid,' says IngerLise, and the rest were painted. The walls were relaid with simple wooden coverings, then painted or, in the case of the main room on the ground floor, papered with a Designers Guild design.

Both Stein and IngerLise like to spend as much time as possible in the garden, making it the most used 'room' in summertime. In winter this haven is replaced by the small library upstairs. 'I am very fond of reading, and we spend a lot of time there in the good chairs, with some good music, a good book and a glass of wine,' says IngerLise.

Ultimately, the real simplicity of the house is that the look that has been achieved has been largely accidental. There was no master plan at the beginning. 'I think it says that we have our own personal style, we are not looking that much to the trends of today, at what happens to be fashionable,' IngerLise explains. 'Actually, I know that "shabby chic" is a trend at the moment, but it never used to be – certainly not ten to fifteen years ago when we first moved here!'

The dining room, in its strong shade of blue, looks through a generous doorway to the comforting green kitchen. The kitchen floorboards have been painted in a warm grey, while those in the dining room have been left natural. All the rooms in the house are painted in strong, earthy colours, which – as here – Stein and IngerLise have not been afraid to mix. In the dining room an assortment of different chairs provide the seating around the long table.

The kitchen window (right) looks on to a spacious, but private, back garden. The most everyday tools (below) are all arranged as if they were props for a still-life painting, revealing the antique dealers' enviable talents in the art of display.

Just as in the kitchen, in the bathroom the shelves of bottles, boxes of soaps and hanging towels seem casual, but are in fact far from disorganized or messy. Instead, each item has its own place and has been arranged with care and consistency. From every angle items are arranged in artistic compositions.

Preceding pages: Pictures line a bright yellow wall leading up to the home office on the first floor. Inside the office the walls have been left to show several layers of old wallpaper and paint that have been worn away over time. A collection of postcards, souvenirs and mementos is arranged on a simple board, making a picture from items that might otherwise be stored away or make the house seem cluttered.

The bedroom, painted in a restful pale blue, and a small reading room next door (opposite), are tidy and organized. Even the clothes hanging directly on the wall (above), in corresponding colours and natural fabrics, manage to look arranged. A board (right) with children's drawings and memories, displayed as an artwork in its own right.

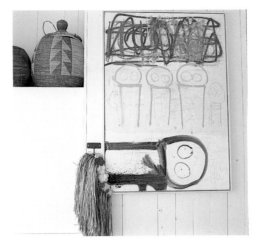

contact addresses

Fiona Bennett
Große Hamburger Straße 25
10115 Berlin
Germany
T 49 30 280 963 30
E info@fionabennett.com
W www.fionabennett.com

Maureen Doherty
Egg
36 Kinnerton St
London
SW1X 8ES
England
T 44 20 7235 0469

Roberto and Karin Einaudi
E re@studioeinaudi.com

Victor Esposito
calle Miguel Gaeta Soler 9
07800 Ibiza
Spain

Mathilde Labrouche
W http://cotepierre.free.fr

Gustav and Ylva Langenskiold
Quartier Gougeas
84580 Oppède
France

Neil Logan and Solveig Fernlund
T 1 212 925 9628
E solveig@fernlundlogan.com
neil@fernlundlogan.com
W www.fernlundlogan.com

Hervé Maury
16 quai de rive neuve
13007 Marseille
France

Lili Nalövi and Jesko Willert
Hochallee 106
20149 Hamburg
Germany
T 49 40 417 043
E atelier@nalovi-willert.de
W www.nalovi-willert.de

Ramon Pujol Roca and David Anadon
Escoda
La Maravilla
Portal de mar, 7
07701 Maó
Menorca
Spain
T 34 971 36 74 74
E mao@lamaravilla.es

Ritva Puolita
Woodnotes
Tallberginkatu 1B
00180 Helsinki
Finland
T 358 9 694 2200
F 358 9 694 2221
E woodnotes@woodnotes.fi
W www.woodnotes.fi

Lena Rahoult
lenarahoult@mac.com

Susanne Rützou
Ravnsborg Tvaergade 5c
2nd Floor
DK 2200 Copenhagen
Denmark
T 45 35 24 06 16
W www.rutzou.com

Mari Saville
Fens Restoration
46 Lots Road
London
SW10 0QF
England
T 44 20 7352 9883

Jérôme Abel Seguin
30, rue Candale
93500 Pantin
France
E jseguinacd@wanadoo.fr
W www.jeromeabelseguin.com

Michael and Marlou Smit
Sissy-Boy
Homeland Biesland 7
1948 RJ Beverwijk
The Netherlands
T 31 0251 361300
W www.sissy-boy.nl

page 1
Pedro Espirito Santo's bathroom
in Portugal.

page 2
The office in Victor Esposito's Ibiza
apartment.

page 4
Looking into Victor Esposito's sitting
room in Ibiza.

All rights reserved.
Published in the United States by Clarkson
Potter/Publishers, an imprint of the Crown
Publishing Group, a division of Random House,
Inc., New York.
www.crownpublishing.com
www.clarksonpotter.com

Originally published in Great Britain by Thames
& Hudson Ltd., London, in 2006.

Clarkson N. Potter is a trademark and Potter
and colophon are registered trademarks of
Random House, Inc.

Library of Congress Cataloging-in-Publication
Data is available upon request.

ISBN-13: 978-0-307-35175-3
ISBN-10: 0-307-35175-0

Printed in Singapore

10 9 8 7 6 5 4 3 2 1

First American Edition